CANDLES
IN THE DARKNESS

COMPILED BY JIM ELDERGILL & NEIL INNES

CANDLES
IN THE DARKNESS

STORIES OF FAITH IN
THE ARMY & ROYAL AIR FORCE

CHRISTIAN FOCUS

Copyright © SASRA 2000

ISBN 1-84550-093-8

10 9 8 7 6 5 4 3 2 1

First published in 2000, reprinted in 2006
by
Christian Focus Publications, Geanies House,
Fearn, Ross-shire, IV20 1TW, Scotland

www.christianfocus.com

Cover design by Alister MacInnes

Printed and bound by
Nørhaven Paperback A/S, Denmark

Unless otherwise stated,
all Scripture quotations taken from the
HOLY BIBLE, NEW INTERNATIONAL VERSION.
Copyright © 1973, 1978, 1984
by International Bible Society.
Used by permission of Hodder & Stoughton Publishers.

Contents

Foreword

Jim Eldergill and I have been associated with the work of SASRA (The Soldiers' & Airmen's Scripture Readers Association) for half a century. We acknowledge with gratitude to God the support and encouragement received from Scripture Reader Evangelists and fellow Christians in the Armed Forces. Both of us have benefited from the ministry of Scripture Readers while serving and in more recent times all those who have contributed to this book have been esteemed colleagues in the task of Forces' Evangelism.

This collection of testimonies reveals something of God's amazing grace in the lives of some of those whose calling it has been, to be witnesses for Christ in the Army and Royal Air Force. Our prayer is that many who read this book will be encouraged to be courageous in their witness for the Lord. While some may come to these pages strangers to a personal experience of Christ, we trust and pray that even through the reading of this book, the reader may be enabled by God's grace to come to know the Lord Jesus Christ as his or her own and personal Saviour. It may be that for some the final chapter 'Steps to Peace with God' will be of particular help. If as a result of reading this book, you require further help, or would like to become a supporter of this ministry, please contact us at our Aldershot Headquarters, or via our web site http://www.sasra.org.uk/

We are grateful to all who have contributed and acknowledge with thanks, the help given in the preparation of the manuscript by Mrs Jean Clayton at SASRA HQ and Mrs Barbara Innes at the Scottish Office. Finally, we appreciate all the encouragement given to us by our publishers Christian Focus Publications and in particular Mr William MacKenzie.

Neil M D Innes
EDINBURGH 2006

Introduction

The Soldiers' and Airmen's Scripture Readers Association

The work of the SASRA, which is a registered charity (No. 235708), started officially in 1838. The objects of the Association are:

To spread the saving knowledge of Christ among the personnel of HM Forces.
To promote Christian Fellowship amongst men and women of all denominations serving in the Army and RAF.

In 1854, the then Soldier's Friend Society received offical recognition, which remains until this day from the then War Office.

Further information concerning the Association and its work may be obtained from our website: **www.sasra.org.uk** or by e-mail: **info@sasra.org.uk** or by writing to SASRA, Havelock House, Barrack Road, Aldershot, Hants GU11 3NP (Tel: **01252 310033**).

Our Royal Day to Remember

I had the privilege of being President of SASRA from July 1985 until 8 May 1999; I look back with enormous pleasure and gratitude to God for that singular experience. One of the highlights must be the unique May 1988 'Our Day' to celebrate one hundred and fifty years of ministry by Scripture Readers. Our gracious Patron was with us for the Service of Re-dedication in the Guards Chapel – what singing there was that day – and the memorable reception afterwards, during which Her Majesty met our Scripture Readers and their wives. The Queen was clearly moved by our front-line workers and asked to meet many more of them than we had originally intended. We presented her with a copy of Brigadier Ian Dobbie's history of SASRA, 'Sovereign Service' which she gladly accepted. At the end of a very special 'Our Day' we went home rejoicing at our great privilege in having been called 'to spread the saving knowledge of the Lord Jesus Christ to the serving members of the Army and the Royal Air Force and their families'. Sovereign Service indeed.

Maj Gen Sir Laurence New

1

ASR Meg Atkinson

Coming from a family of five, Sunday mornings were always a time my parents had to themselves, so, along with my three brothers and sister we were sent to Sunday School. However, I excelled in the area of sport and, at 11 years old I replaced Sunday School with the athletics track. I joined a running club and three nights a week plus Sunday morning you would find me there. Sport in general began to dominate my life. Anything with a stick, ball, or racquet, you name it, I loved it. I even have a trophy for football.

Join the Forces; meet new friends; travel the world; good pay; enjoy all the sport you want. Who could resist such an offer? On leaving school in 1966, I joined the WRAF and commenced my square bashing, as it was 'affectionately' known, in the December. Following initial training, I was sent to St Athan to do my parachute packing course. Service life certainly enabled me to enjoy all the sports and I played for my various units in tennis; net ball; hockey, and athletics. I even completed two parachute jumps!

I was not keen on the usual sort of entertainment,

so very often I was on my own. It was not long before the pull of the crowd won me over and soon I became 'one of the gang'. I was very careful however never to let my guard down in certain areas of life; one being I never indulged in alcohol, having witnessed the tricks played on others with severe consequences.

On my posting to Hullavington in 1967, I found myself sharing a room with Jane. She did something I'd never seen before. She sat and read her Bible openly before others. I was not interested enough to ask her why she read it so faithfully or what it meant to her. She was such a shy quiet person, who did not speak by lip about her faith but she did by her life. I could see that she was different to me.

September 1968 saw me posted to Bruggen, Germany and a few weeks later, Jane followed. Again we found ourselves sharing the same room and I found myself under the influence of this 'religious friend'. The local Scripture Reader John Swan made contact with Jane and through her, I was invited to his house for tea. I met so many young service lads and lasses and found them sincere and friendly. I noticed that they talked about Jesus so personally, as though He was right there with them. To me, He was part of history like Walter Raleigh, who made His mark. I enjoyed being with these people and found myself going back each week to learn more. Truly I had the best of both worlds. Playing regularly in team sports, representing my unit and enjoying this group of people. I began to realise who Jesus really was and what He had done for me in dying on the cross. I knew I was a sinner, my actions told me so. I also knew something was happening to me though I could not have put it into words at that time.

February 13th, 1969 was like any other day to me. It turned out to be like none other because that evening after our regular Bible Study, I had a personal chat with the Scripture Reader which resulted in us getting down on our knees and I asked Jesus to be my Saviour and Lord. History became a reality!

My life's ambition was to join the Police Force on completion of my time in the WRAF, but God had other ideas. During Bible College training, God clearly called me into the ranks of the Scripture Readers and since September, 1974, I have been privileged to share the good news of Jesus Christ with the lads and lasses in the Swindon Area, both RAF and Army. My greatest joy is seeing some enlist in the Army of the Lord and going on to become good soldiers of Jesus Christ.

Meg Atkinson served with the Women's Royal Air Force from December, 1966 to September, 1971. She commenced her work with SASRA as a Lady Scripture Reader in September, 1974.

2

ASR Bob Barbour

In 1963, under the ministry of Scottish Evangelist, Alex Tee, I invited the Lord Jesus Christ into my life as Saviour. A year later I joined the Army, very much against my mother's wishes, because she was concerned that I would not continue with my Christian faith. I praise God for His keeping power all through my Army career.

My first contact with SASRA was in 1965, whilst I was serving in Cyprus. I thank God for men like John Austin and Derek Yarwood, who with his wife Barbara, invited me into their home. Shortly after my return home, I became a SASRA member. In 1969, I was posted to Northern Ireland, where I met my wife Ruth and we have been blessed with three children; Mark; Sharon and Stephen. Stephen was killed in a tragic accident a week after his sixth birthday but we do praise God that he had earlier asked the Lord into his life and for the way He undertook for us during this very trying time. In 1986 I was asked by the late Jim Beggs, if I had thought of becoming a part time Scripture Reader. After much thought and prayer, I believed that this was what God wanted me to do. I applied, was accepted and visited with Jim Beggs who taught me a lot about the work of a Scripture Reader.

At the time of writing, I visit Thiepval Barracks and during the troubles, was priviledged to visit the Maze prison. It is a real joy for me to talk to the lads about the Lord and their need to become Christians. I do praise God for the opportunities given to share the Gospel with these men. It is very encouraging when they ask questions about the Bible and then ask for Bibles and tracts which they promise to read.

For the past sixteen years, I have been privileged to teach boys and girls in the Garrison Sunday School, which I took over from the late Gladys Blackburn. Over the years, God has raised up Godly teachers and Chaplains, who have been a great encouragement to me, both in the work of SASRA and the Sunday School.

In 1997, we knew again the protection of God on our family, when our home was petrol bombed. The damage to the building and the contents was extensive, yet no one was hurt. This made some of the emergency people who dealt with the attack comment that there was someone above watching over the family. This was repeated many times and we give the glory to God. It was so marvellous to receive letters and gifts from so many with the assurance of their prayers. We thank God for our Christian and SASRA family.

Looking back over the years since I became a Christian I can see the hand of God on my life and I thank Him for His numerous blessings to myself and my family. I also thank God for the privilege of being involved in the work of SASRA and trust that I will be able to work for Him for many more years to come.

Bob Barbour served in the Royal Pioneer Corps from August, 1964 to August, 1986. His work as a part-time Scripture Reader with SASRA began in November, 1988.

3

Mr Steven Carter

At age sixteen I was heavily committed to sport, especially water polo. In the midst of this a school friend invited me along to a Saturday evening youth club at a nearby Baptist church. The friendliness of the group caused me to attend, once on a Sunday, over a period of six months. During that time I became aware that the Bible was, and is, an historically reliable document.

One Sunday evening in 1966, I was converted to Christ through the text *Matthew 7:13,14, 'Enter through the narrow gate. For wide is the gate and broad is the road that leads to destruction and many enter through it. But small is the gate and narrow the road that leads to life, and only a few find it.'* The statement was made, 'there is a broad road that leads to destruction and a narrow road that leads to life *and there is no in between!'* My 'in between' refuge disappeared! That night I sought out the preacher and took *John 3:16 'For God so loved the world that He gave His only begotten Son, that whosoever believes in Him shall not perish but have eternal life'* as my basis for acceptance before God.

Since that time God developed a desire in me to serve Him. Following an apprenticeship as a printer, I entered Bible College for three years and then the pastoral ministry for the next eighteen years.

My wife Linda was born of Christian parents on a farm in South Wales. Eventually she left home to study at Agricultural College. She knew a lot about God but did not enjoy a personal relationship with Him. While at college, she started to attend a Youth Fellowship in the town of Usk. It was here that she learned that it wasn't so much her deciding to follow Christ that mattered but rather to turn from sin in repentance and seek God's forgiveness. The Holy Spirit would then do a work in her life. That was nearly thirty years ago. Soon after leaving college, Linda and I were married and the Lord has blessed us with two children, Rebecca and Tim.

We belonged to a SASRA supporting church for a number of years and had prayed for and attended SASRA meetings. In 1995, Courtenay Harris, the then Northern Area Representative, approached and asked us to consider the possibility of ministry with SASRA. Having gone through the selection procedure, we became convinced that God was indeed calling us to work with the Association in its ministry to servicemen and women. Every day we continue to prove the truth of *Philippians 4:6,7 'Do not be anxious about anything, but in everything, by prayer and petition, with thanksgiving, present your requests to God. And the peace of God, which transcends all understanding, will guard your hearts and your minds in Christ Jesus.' God's peace endures!*

Steven Carter has worked as an Area Representative with SASRA since 1996. He is married to Linda and they have two grown up children.

4

ASR Sally Clarke

At the age of twenty eight, I was married with four children and suddenly, I was a widow. The Lord called my husband Billy 'home' at the early age of thirty. This was not the plan that I had for my life but the prophet *Jeremiah 29:11 reminds us that the plans God has for our lives are 'not to harm us, but to give us hope for the future.'*

During those early years of widowhood, we really had to depend on the Lord for so much and yet, of a truth, we can say He never disappointed us once. We took Him at His word and just made all His promises our own ...we named them and claimed them.

At the time of my husband's death, our youngest child Ian was just four weeks old. His Dad had served seven years in the Royal Air-Force so, at the age of twenty two, he thought he would like to try 'service life.'

Now, I did not come from a military family and, as a consequence, knew very little about Army life. However, as a Christian Mother, I was reminded that my late husband had 'met the Lord' whilst in the

RAF and so I felt the same might happen with my dear son. He went to Ballymena, County Antrim, the Depot of the Royal Irish Regiment for initial training which was to last six months. My heart's desire was that he would 'get saved' and be used of the Lord for His glory in the Army.

One morning, I was having a quiet time with the Lord and my thoughts had turned to *Psalm 10 and as I read verse fourteen, a real sense of God's peace descended on me. It read 'but you, O Lord, do see trouble and grief; you consider it to take it in hand. The victim commits himself to you, you are the Father of the helpless.'*

I remember asking God to be with Ian just at that very moment.

A few hours later, the Training Officer, a Major, arrived at my home to tell me that Ian was dead. This was a dreadful shock and, more so, when the Major told me he had taken his own life earlier that morning. (Just hours before I had been praying from *Psalm 10:14*).

This was to be a real trial of my faith! I pondered this dreadful event and what kept coming back to me were the words, 'Satan meant it for evil, but God meant it for good.' I was ill for the next six months but then God started to strengthen me, physically, emotionally and, most importantly, spiritually. In due time, I was able to assume my work with an Insurance Company. There then followed the difficult task of facing up to Ian's inquest. It appeared that he did not like Army life and had requested to leave. However, his request was outside the time limit (he had only four weeks remaining of training) and so he was refused permission to leave. This had been too much for him to cope with!

One morning after re-starting work, I was in need of some encouragement. I found myself perusing God's Word and again my attention was drawn to *Psalm 10:14*. I read this again slowly and the realisation of what God had been telling me on that fateful morning became clear. 'God,' I read, 'Had the matter in hand. He saw Ian's need.

Ian, a victim, had committed himself into the Lord's keeping and, God was assuring me that He was the Helper of my fatherless son.' I claimed this promise of the Lord for Ian and since then, I have had that assurance that my beloved son is with my beloved Lord!!!

As the months following Ian's death passed by, I felt a deepening burden for those lads in the billets, who had shared Ian's last hours on this earth. I felt the need to get alongside them and help them share the burdens they carried, to encourage them and basically to give them a 'listening ear.'

God was to wonderfully answer my prayers and soon a door opened into the work of 'the Mission to Military Garrisons' (The MMG). I was accepted into this work and even then God was making provision for my future. The Insurance Company I had worked with for some twenty two years, agreed to me leaving and also graciously gave me an early pension.

I served two years with the MMG in Cyprus and the Falkland Islands. This was invaluable experience and gave me an insight into military life. In these two years of 'sharing Jesus,' I was to see many service-men/women come to a saving knowledge of Jesus Christ as Lord and Saviour. Whilst away from home, our (SASRA) Area Representative in Northern Ireland, had been writing to me and telling me of the great need for a Lady Scripture Reader in Ulster. When my time was finished with the MMG, I returned home to Northern Ireland and found myself involved with the SASRA monthly Prayer/report meeting. As I listened to the Scripture Readers give their reports, a growing conviction came upon me that I needed to be used in that capacity .. not least among the female soldiers. So, in God's time, I became the first Lady Scripture Reader serving in the Province for over thirty years.

Now, praise the Lord, I have a large family of girls. I cover three camps, Thiepval, Palace Barracks and Kinnegar Camp and I visit these on a weekly basis. I never forget the responsibility we have before God to *'go forth and preach the Word' (Matt. 28:19,20)* and also the great privilege that is mine to visit these girls in their 'homes' (the barrack rooms) and share my faith with them. I invite these girls home frequently for a meal and am over-joyed when on occasions, they accompany me to my 'home' church in Belfast.

The work is daunting but the target is simple. I aim to 'sow the seed of the glorious Gospel in their hearts'.. 'allow the Holy Spirit to bring conviction and conversion'.. and to be there to encourage and exhort as God directs.

Mrs Sally Clarke has served as a Lady Scripture Reader in Northern Ireland since October, 1991.

5

ASR Bob Clayton

It was February 1977 when Jean (my wife) and I repented of our sin and put our complete trust in the Lord Jesus Christ. What a journey it's been since!

We had been married four years and life was becoming increasingly difficult. I had been medically discharged from the RAMC a year before we met and married. Sadly my condition continued. Things were going wrong and there seemed no answer. Even though in our desperate need we looked for God, 'religion' had let us down and we knew it was not the answer. We had recently moved house to Manchester and unknown to us, our neighbours were Christians. The husband's life impressed me so much that I enquired of his faith and church. An invitation was given to attend the little Gospel Hall, through which we both soon committed our lives to Christ. Depression lifted and disappeared and peace came! Our marriage has continued to grow stronger. Life changed radically and with a one year old daughter, Lucy, who suffers from cerebral palsy, we needed all the help and grace that God poured out upon us.

Over the next ten years the Lord prepared us and led us in a miraculous way. We moved again back to the Midlands, where I worked in secular employment for a year, until our 'call' into 'full-time Christian work'. Four years were spent with the Birmingham City Mission, a hard but good training and serving ground, followed by Missionary Bible College in Berwick upon Tweed. The Lord faithfully provided for us. We thought this would be three years of solely academic training. God had other plans and continued to do a wonderful work in our own lives.

Jean and I had been praying for SASRA, never considering the possibility of joining their ranks as an ASR. An impossibility we thought! There were too many obstacles. Approaching our last term of college, we were exercised to contact the then General Secretary of SASRA, Lt Col K Sear, to visit him **ONLY** to obtain greater information so that we could pray more intelligently for the work. That was the start of a long, very thorough process of recruitment, selection, 'calling' and the very definite direction of God. *Proverbs 3:5-6.*

One of the first people we met whilst visiting SASRA's Aldershot HQ in 1985, was Mrs Vera Crofts, the then Prayer Secretary. She asked me where I had served and had I ever come across an ASR? I had spent three and a half years in the army in Aldershot, Keogh Barracks, home and then training camp for medics. I remembered this 'religious' guy popping his head around the door of the TV room one Saturday afternoon, whilst we were watching an England match. I immediately recalled in my mind the tough time we had given him and how, on that occasion, we had told him to 'Get lost!' Vera produced a picture and asked if I recognised the man, to which I instantly replied in the affirmative. She then informed me that the 'religious visitor' we had met that day, was indeed her late Scripture Reader husband, Frank.

Over the years we have become increasingly convinced of the value of Vera and Frank's prayers for that small group of rebellious medics. Today, some twelve years later, I continue as an ASR, to have the opportunity of visiting the same barracks and knocking on the very same doors in order to take the wonderful, unchanging message of the Saviour. Our time so far with SASRA has continued to be a great growing and learning curve. Along the way we have been proving that 'His grace is sufficient' and His provision and enabling always constant. In line with *1 Timothy 1:12, 'I thank Christ Jesus our Lord who has enabled me, because He counted me faithful, putting me into the ministry.'*

Praise Him!

Bob Clayton served in the RAMC from September, 1966 until November, 1969. He began his work with SASRA as a full time Scripture Reader in September, 1986. Bob retired from SASRA in June, 2005.

6

Gen Sir Richard Dannatt
KCB CBE MC

Berlin is a fascinating city and a tremendous posting in which to begin married life. Friday, 11th November 1977, should have been a day no different from any Friday. The morning was unremarkable for both of us; Pippa, my wife, worked at the Kindergarten and I was in and out of my office.

After lunch, Pippa took her sister and a friend off to an art gallery and I returned to my office. The Colonel held his normal Friday conference and my next intention was to meet the RSM and to check the preparations for the Battalion's Armistice Day Service which was to be held at 3.30 p.m. that afternoon. I never met the RSM, nor did I check the preparations for the Service.

Very Seriously Ill
For the next three-quarters of an hour no one saw me. I was lying on the floor of the cloakroom in Battalion Headquarters. My right side was paralysed and I couldn't talk sense.

When a brother officer finally found me, I was rushed with blue lights flashing, to the neurology department of the main German hospital. Some while later Pippa was found, and very gently told that she should not hope for too much. Although in different circumstances, life had stopped for both of us.

This part of the story is hers and not mine. Pippa told me afterwards that in the car with the Padre on the way to the hospital, her only thought was how sorry she was for whoever was to be assigned the task of telling her that I had died! I did not die, nor had God the slightest intention of letting me die. I knew throughout that I would live, and I had no doubt whatsoever that I would make a full recovery but, at that stage I did not know why I felt so sure.

Medically I had all the symptoms of a classic stroke, supposedly unheard of at twenty six and equally strangely, there appeared to be no physical cause for it. Every test that a modern teaching hospital can think of had been tried, and there was no explanation. However, although there was no explanation as to the cause of my collapse, the treatment remained the same, at least four weeks firmly in bed. My mind cleared first, and my speech returned to normal within hours. My right arm loosened up in a few days and my right leg slowly came back to life.

The opportunity to step back for four weeks from the normal bustle and business of life is an opportunity that very rarely presents itself. For me, as alarming as the initial circumstances were, four weeks enforced rest as a spectator on life, rather than as a participant, had enabled me to clear my head and allow God to speak to me.

Although I had been a follower of Christ for several years, I knew that I had only ever given part of my life to Him but kept a part for myself. As I lay in bed recovering I began to reflect that God wanted all of my life, not just part and that He had challenged me about this on occasions in the recent past.

God's Protection

On 7th February, 1973, in very unpleasant circumstances in Belfast at the end of a day of much shooting and people being killed. Two gunmen outflanked the position I had taken up as my Platoon Headquarters. I was briefing one of my Section Commanders on re-deployment plans. My driver was down beside my vehicle as sentry. A hail of bullets leaped down the street. The Corporal and my driver fell on either side of me. My driver later died. I walked away unharmed.

On 17th July, 1975, I was with my Company Commander in a mine clearance operation in South Armagh. We began to go forward to a good location from which we could observe the suspicious object. After a few yards my Company Commander passed me an air photograph, which he suggested I should study rather than go any further forward with him. I stopped and looked at the photograph. Half a minute later and thirty yards away 70lb of commercial explosive detonated. My friend was killed instantly. I walked away unharmed.

On 15th March, 1977, I was driving along a West German autobahn from Berlin to the Hook of Holland. I was going home to get married. It was the small hours of the morning and I was tired. I fell asleep and drove off the autobahn at 70 mph straight into a field. At the point where I went off the road the field and road were absolutely level and flat, two hundred yards further on there was a twenty-foot bank and a wood. I walked away unharmed.

Thus, on three occasions God had shown me His love and His protection and had challenged me to make a complete commitment to Him but on each occasion, I had failed to make the response that He wanted from me. Finally I had to be stopped so that the lesson could be learned. On the fourth occasion I could walk nowhere.

One of the many letters that Pippa and I received from friends when they heard that I had been taken ill was from a very wise experienced Christian from whom Pippa and I had gladly taken advice before. We were delighted by the letter and the practical encouragement it contained. The friend, however, made reference to *Hebrews 12*. I looked it up the next day and realised it to be the key piece in the jigsaw.

> 'My son, do not make light of the Lord's discipline, and do not lose heart when He rebukes you, because the Lord disciplines those whom He loves, and He punishes everyone He accepts as a son... Our fathers disciplined us for a little while as they thought best; but God disciplines us for our good, that we may share in His holiness.'

In my circumstances those six verses are almost the classic example of a blinding flash of the obvious. I had refused to learn the lesson on three occasions in the past, therefore, God had no choice but to take a stick and beat me over the head. The justice of my punishment is almost poetic. How many times in the previous year as Adjutant had I heard the Commanding Officer admonish a soldier for his transgression. Indeed, how often had I done it myself? God had given me a timely taste of my own medicine!

Lessons to be learnt

God's lesson in discipline to me is supremely constructive. Obviously the physical discomfort of collapsing and being paralysed was not trivial, neither was the mental anguish of the first few hours an easy burden for Pippa. However, as the years have gone by and the significance of the lessons to be learnt realised, we are both able to rejoice together and praise God for His mysterious and loving ways.

11th November is the date in the calendar each year when we remember Armistice Day – for it was the 11th hour of the 11th day of November 1918 that the surrender of Germany to end the First World War was announced. A surrender is two things – it is the end of the fighting and the beginning of peace. I discovered that 11th November 1977 was the moment that I stopped fighting with God – only giving Him part of my life – and that it was the moment that I fully committed myself to Him. My passage in *Hebrews 12* ends: *'No discipline seems pleasant at the time, but painful. Later on, however, it produces a harvest of righteousness and peace for those who have been trained by it.'*

I found on that date, that a far better way of life was to commit myself wholeheartedly to Him, to enjoy that peace and purpose in life that only full commitment to Jesus Christ can bring.

At the beginning of March 1978, I returned to work as Adjutant of my Battalion in Berlin, and in November was finally passed as fully fit again.

There can be no end to this story, for the end is the beginning, the beginning of a new life in Christ.

Richard Dannatt, was commissioned into the Green Howards in July, 1971. In June 2004, General Dannatt received a Knighthood in the Queen's Birthday Honours list. He became Commander UKLF (United Kingdom Land Forces) in March 2005. A member of the SASRA Council from 1992, his Presidency of the Association commenced in May, 1999.

7

Brig W I C Dobbie

It has been said that a man cannot take too much trouble in the selection of his grandfather! Behind this frivolous remark lies a kernel of truth and I am deeply grateful for the Godly influence of one of mine. Not only did he pray for me every day for the first 25 years of my life, he drew the first profession of faith out of me as a boy. I have to regard that profession as spiritual conception rather than birth, for my understanding of the Gospel was as shallow as my repentance. When my new Birth occurred in August, 1961, I was greatly aware of His gracious promise, *'I will never leave you or forsake you,'* Hebrews 13:5 and also a release from sin and guilt not previously experienced.

As I write these words, I do so as a man whose sole confidence to stand before a Holy God, rests on the forgiveness won for me by the Lord Jesus Christ when He died on the Cross as my substitute and sin bearer. On that day, God in Christ took upon His own innocent person the just punishment of my sin, rebellion and guilt, so that I might stand before him as an innocent man. For at the Cross, God in His justice displayed His hatred of my sin by punishing it and, in His unquenchable love to a sinner like me, took that punishment on Himself. Thus in His genius, he has satisfied entirely both His justice and His love simultaneously. I write therefore, as an old hymn says as a 'debtor to mercy alone'.

One valuable and practical piece of advice my grandfather gave me was to form the habit of beginning and ending the day with God in Bible reading and prayer. On another occasion he was to say, 'It is good to begin each day by hearing God's opinions before we hear the world's and, to speak with Him before we speak to the world.' The remainder of this testimony is focused on how influential this habit was to be during just one tour of duty and in a particular operational situation.

In 1974, I was appointed to command a Royal Engineer Field Squadron in Germany. On the morning I assumed command, my daily reading was in *Acts 7*, which records the first Christian martyr, Stephen, testifying before the Jewish Council to God's dealings with His servants in Old Testament times. In *verse 9*, Stephen says of Joseph, who had been sold by his brothers into Egypt, '*but God was with him.*' Those words seemed to fit my needs that day and I prayed that they may be true of me in the new responsibilities I was undertaking.

Ten months later, after a difficult start but, aware of a new cohesion in the squadron and some encouraging performances on exercise and on the sports field, I was reading *Genesis 50:24* and was arrested by words this time uttered by Joseph as he died: *'But God will be with you and bring you again to the land of your fathers.'* The first part seemed so similar to the verse I had claimed on assuming command, I naturally wondered why I had been given it that day. That morning I saw the reason. The Commanding Officer called his Squadron Commanders together to tell us that the Regiment would be going to Londonderry in the infantry role in ten months time. I realised what a gracious promise I had been given that morning. We arrived in Londonderry, well trained and prepared. My Squadron was responsible for the security of the City and the Strand – a shopping precinct running north from the City on the west bank of the River Foyle. Our predecessors had had three soldiers murdered by the IRA and were fortunate not to lose at least two more. On about our first evening a gunman opened up with an automatic weapon firing twenty seven rounds over a Landrover in which one of my corporals was patrolling. In the first three months we dealt with most of the incidents which were routine in the experience of units serving in Ulster at that time, including ninety or so bomb incidents, most of which were hoaxes. Then one evening my CO came down to my headquarters to tell me that an informer had let him know that the IRA planned to shoot a soldier at a checkpoint as opportunity provided. By now most of my soldiers were working a seventeen hour day, standing day and night at check points for six hours at a time and, I had no reserves to use as mobile patrols as a counter measure. Whereas I had been confident about my own safety, I had no such confidence for my soldiers. I knelt down by my bed that night to commit this to the Lord but turned in, feeling tense. However, my first waking thought next morning was the opening words of a verse I had learned some years previously from *Isaiah 54:17, 'No weapon that is formed against you shall prosper.'* (NKJV) A great sense of release seemed to flow through me. On a Saturday afternoon shortly afterwards a report came over the squadron radio net that a shot had been fired at a sentry but missed. We carried out a follow up but without success and, soon after this incident, were returning to Germany with every man fit and virtually unmarked and, with the general level of violence in Londonderry lower than for some years. Two days later we heard with sorrow that our successors had lost a soldier at a point where I and my escort had stood for several moments on numerous occasions daily.

It was now time to hand over command of my squadron. At the close of my final address, I gave every officer and soldier a New Testament with the following words printed on the fly-leaf:

'This is a modern translation of a book which has had a decisive influence, especially in our own country, for several hundred years. It tells the story of how God Himself visited the world He made in the person of Jesus Christ, of how and why He died for each one of us personally, of His rising from the dead and of the very best plan for our lives.

Many through reading this book, have come to trust this wonderful person for themselves. Such an experience cannot fail to make men grateful as their lives become enriched and purposeful and, I warmly recommend the reading of this book accordingly.'

It is my testimony that God and His Word are entirely faithful. We neglect both at our peril or, more wisely, we receive them to His glory, to the benefit of others and to our own comfort.

Ian Dobbie was commissioned in the Royal Engineers in November, 1958. He joined the SASRA Council in October, 1976 and became chairman in 1991.

8

ASR Jim Downie

I was born and brought up in the east end of Belfast, one of seven children. My Father died when I was six years old and my Mother was left a young widow, with a large family to care for. Following my Mother's conversion, church played quite a central role in the lives of our family but had little lasting effect on any of us as children. As soon as we reached sixteen, the age at which we no longer had to attend church, most of us sought our own way in the world. For me, this involved becoming embroiled in the uneasy political situation at home and becoming an accomplished young man in the world, trying everything that it had to offer. At the age of eighteen things took a turn as I left college and joined the Army. To have continued at home would have resulted in me ending up either in the graveyard or jail. Life in the military presented me with even greater freedom and I exploited this to the full. I eventually settled into the job and enjoyed promotion, although I still had the reputation of being a hard drinking, hard living individual. It was in Zimbabwe in the early eighties that I met my wife

Debbie. Marriage settled me but a little, even when we had our two daughters, Kirsten and Ceara, I remained very much as I was. Throughout this period I recall a feeling of never seeming to be fulfilled in any real way. It was true I had a lovely family and by this time had reached the rank of Warrant Officer. We enjoyed financial security (despite my gambling) but there was something missing from our lives. It was whilst serving once again in Africa, in the little kingdom of Lesotho, that this was to change. We had started to attend church for the children's sake and not out of any sense of need in our own lives! Debbie was invited to a Bible Study to which she eventually went, with a view of getting them to stop asking her. Within a few months Debbie had accepted Christ and my world was turned upside down! Soon I noticed a change in Debbie's life; a security, a sense of peace, in effect a complete change of direction. I saw in Debbie what I knew to be missing in my own life but, I was not going to turn religious, not me! I had too much to lose. I called the shots in my life, nobody else. I became aware of an internal battle raging within myself, knowing my life was all wrong and in need of some serious help but I would not give in. I sat Debbie down one evening and in total frustration told her she could have me or Jesus but not us both. When I think of my arrogance today it makes me shiver. Within a month my world was thrown into complete confusion. Suddenly the Jim Downie who was so much in control, could no longer control anything. Pride they say comes before a fall and I fell! It is a testimony to God's grace, mercy and great love, that when I reached my knees, He was there for me. When I had tried all my own ways and failed; when I thought I had lost everything; when I was broken, only then did I cry out to a God whom I had cursed and hated and asked His forgiveness. Then He touched me, deep, deep down inside.

Some have since said to me that my turning to Christ was only a crutch and I can see how they might think that. For me, there was so much more involved. The old Jim Downie would never have bent the knee. I fought with God, like a wild horse, I kicked and turned. I never needed a crutch, I needed a Saviour. First I needed to be broken and, bless His glorious Name, He did just that and drew me to Himself.

As a family our whole focus has changed. Our two daughters have come to faith in Christ. We are now a family in Him and it is as a family we now seek to serve Him with SASRA.

Jim Downie joined the Royal Irish in July, 1972 and served until February, 1994. His ministry with SASRA as a Scripture Reader commenced in March, 1995. In 2005, Jim resigned from SASRA to answer God's call to a pastoral ministry.

9

ASR Berenice Ducker

I grew up in Wandsworth in South West London in a secure and loving family. I always remember my parents spending lots of time with us. Dad's day off was particularly exiting for my sister and me because he would invariably make us his speciality mashed potato and fried egg and give us pocket money to buy sweets. Mum was the one who used to talk about Jesus. At that point, Dad seemed uninterested in religion.

I joined the RAF in 1990 and trained as a police dog handler shortly after my parents moved to Chelmsford in Essex. I was not a Christian during my time in the RAF and it was only after my conversion in 1997 that I found out about the work of SASRA. I did not meet a Scripture Reader whilst I was serving and wonder what my reaction would have been had I come in to contact with one. I did go to church when I was younger but stopped going after my first confirmation lesson because I really did not understand the bible. Although I have to say, I did believe that God existed.

It was involvement in Sea Cadets that gave me a taste for life in the Armed Forces and my decision to join the RAF was based on the fact that they had started to recruit women police dog handlers. So, as a naive nineteen year old, I joined up. It didn't take long before I started to drink quite frequently. I also engaged in casual relationships and quickly developed a very selfish attitude to living.

Even though I continued to believe in Jesus he made no real difference to the way I lived. However after leaving the RAF I did start to consider how I had behaved whilst I was serving and felt it necessary to go for an HIV test for peace of mind. Having to wait for the results was the most traumatic 24 hours of my life. If the test result came back positive I couldn't bare the thought of infecting someone else so I intended to commit suicide. I spent all night crying out to God that if he gave me a second chance I would promise to live the way he wanted. I collected the result and was told it was negative. I remember thinking 'I've made this promise to God that I have now to honour.'

About this time I went for behavioural counselling but I remember each time I walked into the counsellor's room I felt I should really be in a church speaking with a vicar. I then went on a retreat to a friary where I had counselling with a lovely sister who kept giving me bible verses to read but the bible still made no sense to me. It was only when I made a decision to go to university at the age of 27 that I discovered that I could have more than just a knowledge of who Jesus was. I could actually have a personal living relationship with him.

I decided to join the University of Bangor canoe club and had gone to mid-Wales with a group of students for the Welsh inter-university canoeing competition. During the trip, I discovered that there was a Christian named James on the team. On the return journey home he sat in front of me on the coach and I began to quiz him about his faith. By the end of the journey we agreed that he would take me to the next Christian Union meeting which was held on campus. On the night I went the group were singing the song 'You laid aside your majesty' and I knew exactly what the words meant.

At the end of the evening, James introduced me to his sister Jenny and we immediately became friends. A few days later I was introduced to her housemates three students called Jo, Emily and Sam. What I noticed about these people is that they cared for each other. They would take it in turns to cook for each other and would often bake cakes to celebrate someone's birthday or other occasions. I was often invited round to have tea with them and within a few weeks, I had moved into their spare room. It didn't take me long before I started to question them on their faith. Then one night I asked Jo how I could become a Christian. She simply said 'you have to ask God for forgiveness and put your faith in Jesus.' So that night I went into my bedroom, closed the door and did just that.

A few months later, I went to a Christian Union mission that was being held on campus. When people were challenged to come to the front to accept Jesus as their saviour, I walked up to the front. I suppose this was a sort of confirmation and public declaration of what I had already done when I spoke to God in my bedroom that night.

It wasn't long before I started to think back to my days in the RAF and I started to pray for opportunities to share the Gospel with service personnel. After leaving university I moved back to Chelmsford. During one of my trips to the local Christian bookshop in Chelmsford I picked up a magazine to take home to read. When I got back home I opened it up to find a flyer with the words SASRA 'Personal Evangelism Amongst the Forces.' I knew then that my experiences in the RAF were for a purpose.

I contacted SASRA and, after the application process was complete, I started working for them in August 2002. My first taste of the work was at the Edinburgh Tattoo where I met several of my new colleagues. I was used as a guinea pig for SASRA at London City Mission where I attended their 4½ month long missionary probationers course. I then spent 6 weeks with Scripture Reader Meg Atkinson at RAF Lyneham before I was posted to Lincolnshire to work with the RAF alongside Scripture Reader Alistair Stewart until his retirement 6 months later. Now, I am the only SASRA Scripture Reader in the Lincoln area

A scripture verse that has always meant a lot to me is *Acts 17:26-28*

'From one man he made every nation of men, that they should inhabit the whole earth; and he determined the times set for them and the exact places where they should live. God did this so that men would seek him and perhaps reach out for him and find him, though he is not far from each of us.'

This verse shows me that God already knew the direction my life would take and the mistakes I would make. He knew that I would eventually seek him, reach out for him and find him. He knew where and with whom best to place me and he knew that it would lead me to finding him.

Berenice Ducker served in the WRAF from July, 1990 until February 1993. She commenced her work as a Scripture Reader with SASRA in August, 2002.

10

ASR John Dunbar

I was brought up in a non-Christian home by parents who were very loving and kind but, had the idea that Christianity was for children and, as you grew up you grew out of this childish fad. The first signs of God leading me was when my friends said that they were joining the Life Boys at the Mission around the corner. At eight years of age, I begged my mother to let me go with them. I came to love the Christian folk at the Shaftesbury Mission and could sense that they loved and prayed for me. We had to go to Sunday School and I began to be grounded in the Word of God. On being promoted to the Boys Brigade at twelve years of age, I found myself exposed to a weekly Bible Class. Our leader was a very godly man, whose face shone like Moses' face, when he had been with God. As a member, I was invited with others, to a special service. The Gospel was preached by a man from Tonypandy. I was now 18 years of age and for the first time in my life I began to feel guilty of sin. I went to the preacher. He pointed me to the Lord Jesus Christ and we knelt down and I confessed my sin.

Within a few days, in April, 1951, I was called up for National Service to Catterick Camp. I had never been away from home before and was very shy. One thing the preacher had taught me was that I must confess the Lord Jesus Christ before men. I had thought about this and decided that I would pray in the Nissen Hut despite thirty soldiers with me. I waited until nearly lights out and plucked up courage. The room went very quiet. Then I heard someone say 'If he wants to pray it's no skin off our nose'. Then a pair of boots were thrown at me and landed just by my side, but it was just high spirits. It was not long before a young man in that group came to know Jesus as his Saviour. I had the joy of praying with him over a Table Tennis game. He was genuine. The following Sunday, I had my first meeting with a Scripture Reader, Victor Leinster. His wife fed us well and we were taken to the United Board Church. We had a lively home fellowship with testimonies, good singing and a study of the Tabernacle in the Wilderness. This was the most interesting study I had ever had. Victor had a model of the Tabernacle and pointed out that there was so much teaching involved. I was impressed by the knowledge this Reader had and felt I would never be able to know my Bible like that.

Later I was posted to Germany. A small group of three started a SASRA fellowship in the YMCA. We visited the Royal Fusiliers; 14th Field Ambulance and my own Regiment. God blessed this and we had fifteen soldiers come to the fellowship and two officers from the Fusiliers. When I was demobbed I went back to the Mission and worked as a counsellor at the Billy Graham Crusade. I met and married Doreen, the best lady in Britain, had a large family and supported SASRA by prayer, gift and attendance at the 'OUR DAY' meetings.

One day I received a standard letter pointing out the number of camps that were not being visited for lack of workers. Because of this the Council were considering appointing part time Readers. My daily reading that day, contained *2 Corinthians 4:4-5*. I knew I had received a call from God. An interview was arranged at Headquarters but I failed the test. Being convinced of my call, I studied, re-applied six months later and was accepted. My desire was to work at RAF Northolt but I was appointed to Mill Hill. That is how it all began. *Galatians 6:9. 'Let us not be weary in well doing: for in due season we shall reap, if we faint not.'* Praise God.

John Dunbar served in the 10th Royal Hussars from April, 1951 to April, 1956. His work as a part time Reader with SASRA began in London in 1968.

11

The late Maj Gen Ian G C Durie CBE

I write this as I am about to complete the transition from soldier in the Army of the Queen (which gave me enormous pleasure and cause for gratitude to God for 32 years from start to finish) to full time service in the Army of the Lord, where I have also served for many years through my military career.

As a boy, thanks to a believing mother, I cannot remember a time when I did not trust in Christ as my personal Saviour. This faith was however a dimly glowing and private affair and, I guess that it was of little use to God or me and of even less use to those around me. In fact it took the ministry of some good praying ladies in our village outside Plymouth, while I was four thousand miles away on a six month operational tour in Belize, Central America, to lead my wife Janie to the Lord. Up to this point Janie had half believed, turning to God only when she felt the need, which was not often. When I returned, the burning faith she had suddenly been given put me to shame and I humbly begged the Lord's forgiveness and, made a solemn re-commitment of my own life.

In fact, as we both blossomed in a full Trinitarian faith (where before I had been wholly ignorant of and, had completely ignored the person and activity of the Holy Spirit), we both now testify. 'Janie's conversion was the best thing that ever happened to us.'

There is so much that I could tell of the work of the Lord in and around our lives from that point, but I will restrict myself to something of the Lord at work in the Gulf War. I had the great privilege and responsibility as a soldier, of commanding the ten units and eight thousand men and women of the 1st (UK) Armoured Division Divisional Artillery Group in that conflict. I came to that command confident that I was appointed and prepared professionally as fully as I could have asked and, that I was anointed and prepared spiritually by the same hand. I had sought to leave the Army five years earlier for full time Christian work, as my time in command of 29th Commando Regiment Royal Artillery (the Gunner Commandos) was drawing to a close – but God's plan was otherwise. I stayed on through a series of promotions and appointments which thoroughly prepared me for the military task I faced in the Gulf. At the same time my spiritual life deepened as I practised daily the spiritual disciplines of prayer, Bible reading and Christian fellowship. As a result, in November, 1990, when the 1st Armoured Division was mobilised for the Gulf, as I was called back from leave at the Lee Valley Christian Conference Centre in North Devon, I had revealed to me in a special and personal way that whatever might happen to me physically, Janie (who had been suffering for nearly a year from a very severe bout of depression and, who was now understandably anxious about our future) was directly in the hands of our Lord Jesus Christ.

In the Gulf, as the preparations went on apace and I was concerned, as a senior commander in the Division and known as a Christian, that we should be engaged in doing what was right – a just war. The operation seemed to me, at a rational level, to meet fully the criteria for the Just War and, on that basis, I was happy to proceed. Nevertheless, I needed to **KNOW** that this was right. In mid January, 1991, after several days of prayer, the Lord answered me in the words of *Psalm 131*. This short, perhaps obscure, three verse Psalm had been constantly coming before me two months earlier, as I meditated on the Psalm each day at Lee Abbey. As I had prayed and puzzled over it then, the words made no sense in that context – but in Saudi Arabia the words that came to me (1) answered my prayer. It was my job to get the Divisional Artillery into battle and leave the Lord to worry about the great affairs.

Then with confidence that I was prepared, my family were safe in our Saviour's hands and, that the cause was with God, we went some weeks later into battle. In the early hours of the morning of Sunday, 24th February, 1991, as the land battle was about to begin, I sat huddled in one corner of my command post, reading my daily portion of Scripture. All my family used then the Scripture Union 'Alive to God,' daily Bible reading notes. The set reading for that day was the well known Psalm for those in peril *Psalm 91*! I could scarce believe my eyes as I read the words (and the reader should read the whole Psalm to see the effect it had on me):

'.....His faithfulness will be your shield and rampart.
You will not fear the terror of night ...
nor the pestilence that stalks in the darkness,
nor the plague that destroys at midday.
A thousand may fall at your side, ten thousand at your
right hand,
but it will not come near you.
You will only observe with your eyes
and see the punishment of the wicked.'

I gave thanks to God, not as a promise for my own safety (I had only to read on to verse ten ... *'No disaster will come near your tent'* ... and reflect on the fact that I was only in my command post at that hour, because my tent had just blown away!), but for the eternal promise that the words contained and, the knowledge that Janie at home and, our daughter at university, would that awful day, be reading those same words and would be reassured by them. In the event, the pestilence and plague of chemical and biological weapons that had appeared to be such a threat to the Allied Armies, were not used and, the destruction of the Iraqi Army was terrible, whilst our own casualties were extremely light.

After the Allies had freed Kuwait, I told the troops of the Divisional Artillery Group as I went round them, in the words of Joshua to the Israelite Army after the conquest of Canaan (2) *'It was the Lord your God who fought for you.'* This is what I believe to this day but, what did I learn that was new? I saw the tremendous effort it took to transform the British Army from a peacetime garrison force in Germany, preparing for the unlikely event of an attack by the Warsaw Pact armies, to a fighting force capable of taking the battle to the enemy in a distant and unexpected battlefield. I just wonder if the church militant here on earth, 'the Army of the Lord,' thinks too much of the comforts of peacetime soldiering and, too little of the battle that it has to prepare for and fight against, a worse enemy than we faced in the Gulf?

'My heart is not proud, O Lord, my eyes are not haughty; I do not concern myself with great matters or things too wonderful for me. But I have stilled and quieted my soul' (Psalm 131:1, 2).

'It was the Lord who fought for you' (Joshua 23:3).

'O Israel, put your hope in the Lord both now and for ever more' (Psalm 131:3).

Ian Durie was commissioned into the Royal Artillery in July 1964. He rose to the rank of Major General and became Director of Royal Artillery before leaving the Army to enter fulltime ministry in the Church of England. Ian served in parishes in London and Salisbury prior to his death as a result of a road accident in Romania on 20th April, 2005. At the time of his death, he was a member of the SASRA Council, Chairman of the Military Ministries International Missionary Society and studying for a PhD on the theology of the 'Just War'. Ian is survived by his wife Janie and daughter Emily.

12

Mr Jim Eldergill

A young soldier apprentice was travelling back to camp after a summer holiday. Looking up to the site of the Christian camp where he had spent the last few days, he recognised his sin; his need of repentance and the worth of the Saviour, and simply knelt in the compartment of the Torbay Express and received the Lord Jesus Christ as his Saviour and Lord. That was the start of an adventure which was to last. Over the years of service within the Army, despite his many mistakes the Lord never let him down. He was active as a branch secretary, in his local church when serving in the UK and all the time a serving member of SASRA. Married to a super Christian girl (they celebrated their Ruby wedding in '97), he left the service after 17 years and trained as a teacher. Finishing as a RE Department head in '85 he spent the next few years as a full time worker with his church until in '89 was appointed as the Area Rep for SASRA in the South West. During this period of time they were blessed with five children and 11 grandchildren. It is in the looking back that one is made aware of the tremendous grace of our Lord Jesus Christ. We thank Him for His keeping power. The way in which over the years many of the rough edges have been knocked off (many more still to go) but above all the tremendous sense of security as you realise that you are in the safe keeping of an Almighty God who wants only the very best for you. We have had our share of emotional upset, sickness and loss; and the other misfortunes that come your way but the knowledge of His sustaining love is the bedrock on which you can settle and know His peace and presence. I give thanks to Him that He has been so faithful. I am blessed beyond measure in the work that I now do. An opportunity to travel and meet so many lovely people and with the added bonus of being able to speak about my Saviour. Pat & I thank Him for our life together and the blessings we have experienced and trust Him for whatever still lies ahead of us. Confident that He will never let us down and that we can await His coming or call with quiet anticipation.

Jim Eldergill joined the Royal Engineers in 1949 and served in the Regular Army until 1967. Throughout this time he was linked with the Association as a SASRA member. He began his work as the South West of England Area Representative in July, 1989. Jim retired from SASRA in May 2001.

13

ASR Bob Elliot

My family links with SASRA go back to the last century when my Grandfather used to provide hospitality for a British Army Scripture Reader in his home in Cahir, Co Tipperary, Eire.

I was brought up in a Christian home and made a profession of faith when I was twelve years old. At the age of sixteen, I joined the RAF, where I was helped by a Christian instructor at Hereford. From there I went to RAF Wyton where ASR Bob White (and his wife Kitty) greatly encouraged me as a young Christian. As time went on I realised what Jesus Christ meant to me. He had saved me from my sins and now gave me a great love for the Bible and prayer.

I was further helped by ASR's Ken Hepworth, Gerald McClelland and Mel Moodie who was the final Scripture Reader that I had contact with whilst still serving in the RAF. In 1980 I was posted to RAF Brawdy in Wales with the sole intention of finishing my time in the RAF as quickly as possible and going home to settle in Ireland. God had other plans however, as it was here that I met my wife to be, Anne. We were married in 1981 and God blessed us with three sons, Gareth, Jamie and Timothy, all in the space of three years. God also led me into becoming a part time Scripture Reader to Brawdy, working first with the RAF and American Navy and then with the different Army Regiments that have been stationed there.

In July 1996 a great tragedy came to our family, in the loss of our thirteen year old son Jamie, who died as a result of coming into contact with a car not far from our home. We were upheld in prayer throughout the time of Jamie's accident and hospital stay by so many of the SASRA family throughout the world, that it was like being literally held in the palm of God's hand. Since Jamie's home-call ten years ago, God has proved Himself faithful in all things, keeping us as a family through good and bad times. This has been a great trial in our lives and still continues to give us moments of overwhelming sadness.

Despite having suffered this loss, I thank God for His daily leading in my SASRA ministry of preaching the Gospel to Servicemen and women. My wife Anne has her own craft shop, 'Creative Inspirations' which has flourished with God's blessing.

I still thank God for leading me into SASRA and calling me to the work of preaching the Gospel to servicemen and women.

Bob Elliott served in the Royal Air Force from September, 1969 to November, 1982. His service with SASRA as a part time Scripture Reader began in April, 1983.

14

ASR Lily Frampton

The first time I heard of The Soldiers' and Airmen's Scripture Readers Association was in Belfast many years ago, when I attended a meeting at which a Local Representative from the work gave a report on its activities. That night I received a SASRA collecting drum but sadly, the Association did not benefit financially, owing to the fact that I wasn't a Christian. Not having any interest, I gave it no further thought. Little did I know how all that was to change and, how the Lord was silently planning my future even though I had no thought of Him at the time. That future was to involve my salvation and an affiliation with SASRA which has lasted down the years.

In my early life Church and Sunday School played an important part. My three sisters and I were sent every week to local services. All too soon school days gave way to adolescence and then adulthood, when with relief, I left behind my need to accept Christ into my life. Faithful teaching and preaching of the Word of God had become irksome to me and I wanted freedom from it. I had become very friendly with a girl who lived near me called Annie; that was until she came and told me that she had accepted Christ as her Saviour. To say I was horrified was putting it mildly! I felt that Annie had brought our friendship to an end – not so! God in His wisdom continued His plan. I later married Annie's brother Ted and soon had a son. While my friendship with her didn't end, I became the most miserable person imaginable. Why? Because the teaching from Sunday School days and Annie's witness made me feel guilty and, in turn rebellious. Poor Ted! One night he said, 'You have become very hard to live with – I think you should go up to that hall you've been attending. Perhaps they can do something for you and if you don't go, I'll take you.' I should explain that Annie had persuaded me to attend the meetings in the hall which I enjoyed, until the preaching started. I went to the hall that night as Ted's miserable wife and came home a changed person, having had the Scriptures explained to me – a new creature in Christ Jesus. Ted's only comment was 'don't preach at me!' I didn't, but prayed with the other Christians for him and one Sunday, he came to the Hall. He was thoroughly uncomfortable with the Gospel and told himself that it was only the atmosphere – he would be all right when he got to the shipyard the following day. Two weeks later he was back in the Hall having no money to go gambling and, that night the preacher spoke on *Proverbs 29:1 'He that being often reproved and hardeneth his neck shall suddenly be cut off and that without remedy.'* He told me later that he sobbed his way to the cross but couldn't remember what he prayed. Whatever it was God said 'Amen' to it and, when he rose from his knees, he was no longer in his sin, he was a new creature (*2 Cor.5:17*) and, this wonderful assurance never left him.

The change in Ted's life was astonishing, a complete turnaround. Our son Malcolm, when he was six, asked me, 'Mum, am I a Christian?' I said, 'No, the Bible says that all are sinners no matter how young or old.' That night, 4th March, 1949, the three of us knelt by the fireside and Malcolm received Christ as his Saviour. This was a great encouragement to Ted and I because the lad must have seen the change in our lives and wanted what we had. So the Lord gave us household salvation. How good He was to us.

The next big thing was for Ted to get to know the Word of God and, God was ready for that. The day after he was saved he went into work and, as usual someone came up to sell him a sweepstake ticket. When he told the chap he was finished with all that, it went round the blacksmith's shop like wildfire. 'Big Frampton's saved – we'll give him a week!' As a result of that, one of the other chaps came to him and invited him to a little Bible study group held in the lunch hour. He went and they said, 'Welcome, brother, we are studying Hebrews' and gave him a Bible. He didn't know where Hebrews was and said that at that time, the Bible was as black on the inside as it was on the outside. The men were very patient and helpful to him and he gleaned great help from them. At home, I remember him praying, 'Lord, I don't know this book, please teach me' and He did. Ted developed a technique at work to help him learn texts from Scripture. He chalked the first letter of each word on a huge ship's boiler and, as he got the boilers ready for Lloyds' inspection, he would memorise them. At every opportunity, he was reading the Word and seeking to apply it to his life. It was a treasure trove and he kept discovering new things about the Lord and about His second coming. This really excited him – he had never heard anything like it.

We are told in the Word that the devil can come as an angel of light (*2 Cor.11:14*) and that we should be vigilant. He came to Ted in a very subtle way. Ted had never gone back to drinking or gambling. When the Lord saved him, he was transformed. However, at this time when he was discovering the Word of God and enjoying it, he also discovered oil painting and began to paint scenes on shells, then a fire screen and a painting of the Antrim Coast Road. Soon he was going to bed very late, because after returning from meetings, he would pick up his brush and do so again very early the next morning. Then one day it hit him, he was neglecting the Word of God and it was beginning to show. However Ted was soon back on course and the Lord taught him so well that when years later Colonel Clarke, General Secretary of SASRA, told him he had done very well in his oral and written exams for work in the barrack rooms and asked him what Bible College he had attended, Ted replied, 'St Mary's'. 'Oh', said the Colonel, 'is that in Ireland?' 'No', said Ted, 'it's in the New Testament, *Luke 10:39*.' Afterwards he confessed to me that he had been a bit forthright but, dear Colonel Clarke was a deeply spiritual, humble man. Some years later, when Colonel was called Home to be with the Lord, Ted had the privilege of speaking at his funeral service.

Our coming into SASRA was to have far reaching consequences for us. Having never been further than across the Irish Sea, a whole new vista now opened up in service for the Lord.

Our first posting was to Catterick for four years, where God called me to work among Service girls. Next came Singapore where I proved the Lord, when at the age of sixteen after a short illness, He suddenly called our son Malcolm to heaven. At that time Ted's poignant comment was 'The Lord took the best member of the team.' That was when Ted and I found that the Lord not only **saves** but **keeps**. At the end of our term abroad, we were posted to London and since this is my personal testimony, I feel constrained to write something which isn't widely known in order to illustrate God's keeping power. When we were settled in London, the child we were expecting arrived – stillborn. Only God was able for this situation and He did not fail. We experienced His blessing in London and all our other stations right through to retirement, when in spite of all God's love, care and concern in the past, I worried where we were to live. Ted, forever a tower of strength said to me, 'Do you think that God who has looked after us all the years since He saved us, is now going to give us a push and say 'get on with it?' The Lord did indeed have a further plan for us. He provided a wonderful home in the shape of a little cottage in Hampshire. It was there along with so many friends with whom we shared fellowship down the years, we celebrated our 50th wedding anniversary. We enjoyed eighteen happy and fruitful years in the cottage before Ted was suddenly called into God's presence while we were on a holiday in Belfast. Only one word can describe how I felt – devastated! I mentioned at the beginning that the Lord was planning our way – this was also part of His plan. He surrounded me with loving friends who took care of the funeral arrangements. He proved *2 Corinthians 12:9* to me, '*My grace is sufficient.*' He also enabled me to return to the cottage, to village life and friends and, at low points, He takes me back in my memory to the night He saved me. He reminds me that while Ted and Malcolm have 'arrived,' I am still on the journey. My prayer is, that I may know more of Him for what remains of the journey, as I thank Him for coming into my life all those years ago. My testimony in brief is, '*I love the Lord because He has heard my voice.*' *Psalm 116:1.*

Lily Frampton served alongside her husband Ted as a Lady Scripture Reader. They began their full time ministry with SASRA in 1954 and retired in 1978. Ted was called Home to be with the Lord in August, 1996

15

ASR David Gibson

I was born on 28th January, 1938 in Fintona, Co Tyrone, Northern Ireland, one of fourteen children. The Gibson Clan were encouraged to go along to Sunday School. It was whilst attending the Gospel Hall in Fintona that at the age of nine I asked Jesus into my heart. I was teased by many, including children from the folk at the Hall. I did not grow but became a camouflaged Christian. At fifteen I joined the Junior Leaders and graduated into man-service with the Inniskillen Fusiliers in August 1955.

I had one saved brother, Bob, who lived in Sheffield. It was through him and his wife that I came to real faith in the Lord Jesus Christ. During my early years as a Christian, Captain May was a great encouragement to me. After my initial time in the Army was at an end; I had reached the dizzy heights of Sergeant at twenty; I decided to try civvy street. I went to live with my saved brother in Sheffield. It was whilst at a youth rally in a Gospel Hall in Sheffield that I met Joan.

She was born on 28th October 1943 in Darnall,

Sheffield. Her parents brought her up to go to Sunday School and live a good clean life. She is the youngest of three children. Having left school at fifteen she began working as an office worker and eventually as a secretary and typist. On reaching the age of sixteen, she went out with a young man who was in the Army and going to Singapore. He was very soon contacted by the Scripture Reader out there, 'Ted Frampton' and came to faith in the Lord. On returning to the UK, he befriended Brian and Pauline Savage. They took Joan to a Billy Graham Crusade in Manchester where she gave her life to the Lord. That was June 1961. Ted and Lily Frampton had continued to pray for the salvation of this 'unsaved girlfriend'. The boyfriend was to be a ship that passed in the night and, it was to be over a year later when she met 'the light of her life'. She was introduced to me as the man who was going to be a Scripture Reader! That was not to be until 18 further years had passed. Six months later I realised that the Army was the place for me, so back I went to the depot in Northern Ireland to re-enlist in the 1st Btn Royal Inniskillen Fusiliers. Joan and I were married on 19th September 1964 in Cemetery Road Gospel Hall, Sheffield. In our first year of marriage we had three postings. This was to set the trend for most of our married life.

During our service we came into contact with many Scripture Readers. It was the testimony of these special people that was to lay the foundation for our later calling. Frank and Vera Crofts were to become special friends during our time at RMA Sandhurst until 1969.

In January 1980, having served 26 years with the

Army, we finished with the TA in York. We retired into civvy street from there. My day job was as a CCF Instructor with Trent College in Long Eaton, Nottinghamshire. It was whilst there that I came part time into the work of SASRA and visited RAF Newton twice a week. Richard had attended nine schools in his life and we promised him he would finish his school days at one school. However, before Richard was sixteen I had an urgent call to full time service with SASRA. I responded to that call and commenced my three months training before Richard had left school. God's timing is always perfect and by the time I had finished my training, Richard had left school. In August 1982 we were posted to Lincoln and later in 1990 to our final posting in Catterick, from where we retired in October 1998. We have seen many come to faith in the Lord, but it has been through God's faithfulness that we are still seeing these going on with the Lord. The Lord not only saves but he also keeps. Praise His Name!

David Gibson joined the Army in March, 1953. He served as a regular soldier in the Royal Enniskillen Fusiliers and the Royal Irish Rangers until January, 1980. His service with SASRA commenced as a part time Reader at RAF Newton in February, 1980. In 1982, he became a full time Scripture Reader, in which capacity he served until his retirement in 1998. David is married to Joan and they have three grown up children; Richard, Sarah and Helen, all of whom are married. They have four grandchildren; Nathan, Nicholas, Alice and Benjamin.

16

Mr Matthew Glass

I was born in Northern Ireland, and it was here whilst living with my Grandparents that I came to know Jesus Christ as my personal Lord and Saviour. They were fine Christians, and a great example to me. Indeed, I have vivid memories of my dear Grandfather regularly reading God's word in his favourite armchair. When I came to live with my Grandparents at the age of twelve, I had no knowledge of God's love for me; that He had died for my sins; or that I could have a personal relationship with Him, which would one day culminate in His very presence.

My Grandparents prayed for me every day and encouraged me to go to Third Presbyterian Church in Portglenone on a Sunday morning, and to an afternoon Sunday school and evening meeting at the Craigs Mission Hall. My Grandfather and I would walk some 3 miles to the evening meeting together. I also went of my own volition to a Monday meeting at Rasharkin Gospel Hall and to a Friday meeting at Ballywatermoy Gospel Hall. Consequently, my knowledge of God's precious and holy word increased in leaps and bounds. Indeed, on one occasion at Sunday school, my class was challenged to learn the *119th Psalm* by heart, and two of us took up the challenge. A good number of months later and after constant repetition at home, I saw the challenge through (all 176 verses!). I remember it well, and during one afternoon in October 1971, (in the words on the flyleaf of my presented Bible), I perfectly recited the *119th Psalm*. Numerous verses of Scripture were also learnt at the Gospel Hall meetings, and many of them are still firmly fixed in my memory.

In *Psalm 119* we read: *"The unfolding of Your words gives light..."*, and as I was progressively exposed to God's word, I increasingly became aware that I did not have a personal relationship with God. Although I'm not sure of the exact date (I believe that it was during 1972), I remember the day as if it were yesterday. My teacher was absent, and the Superintendent took the lesson reading from *2 Timothy 3, "But realise this, that in the last days difficult times will come ..."* As he read this chapter, I remember the sudden realisation that dawned, in that if I were to die that night, I knew that I would not go to heaven. The lesson ended and my class returned to the rear of the Mission Hall to sing the final hymn.

Before the hymn was announced, I heard the Superintendent say: "If anyone wants to become a Christian, stay behind." The instant he said that, I distinctly remember hearing a loud voice utter the words, "say yes", but only I could hear it. Since this was a completely new experience for a 14 year old, I was not sure what I should do, and as the hymn was being sung the 'voice' had now become a whisper, constantly repeating "say yes". During the penultimate verse I made a conscious decision that I would say yes – the 'voice' stopped.

I went forward at the end of the hymn and down into the rear room, where I asked God to forgive me for all my sin, to come into my heart and life and to become my personal Lord and Saviour. I walked home and told my Grandparents that I'd become a Christian.

I joined the Royal Air Force (RAF) at the age of 16½, and after initial and professional training was posted to RAF Waddington in Lincolnshire. On my first Sunday after the morning service, the Chaplains' Assistant, Miss Ann Macleod, invited me to an afternoon SASRA meeting, in the home of ASR Derek and Heather Brooks. So began my long association with SASRA, and I became a member when I was 17. As a young Christian a long way from home, I was so thankful for the tremendous fellowship and teaching that SASRA provided, and I am greatly indebted to them. I attended my first SASRA rally in Lincoln during 1975, and so began my long friendship with ASR Brian and Janet Henagulph and family. Although I enlisted in the RAF as an incredibly shy individual, yet by God's grace, 10 years later I was a Sergeant.

My next link with the SASRA family was during 1976, when ASR Bob and Barbara Hodson assumed responsibility for Lincolnshire. As I got to know them, they invited me to spend – what would become the first of numerous weekends in their home. Since at that time I was sharing a room with five other chaps, this was an enormous privilege for me to have my own room, even if just for two days. Christian hospitality is of fundamental importance. It was a real joy for me during those early days to lead one of my roommates to the Lord.

Throughout my RAF career I always endeavoured to support the RAF Chaplains, be it in the congregation, or as a Sunday school teacher, Superintendent, youth worker, or Preacher. Indeed, during my Germany tours I was privileged to take many services for the RAF Chaplains, at RAFs Laarbruch, Wildenrath and Brüggen.

A pivotal point in my RAF service occurred when I returned from RAF Laarbruch in Germany during March 1990 and was posted to RAF Catterick in North Yorkshire and attached to the RAF Regiment. (It was here that I appreciated the fellowship of ASR David and Joan Gibson.) During November of 1990, 51 Squadron RAF Regiment deployed to Saudi Arabia (Dhahran), on what was Desert Shield, and would become Desert Storm. We prepared for war, and during the conflict Iraqi Scud missiles frequently attacked our base.

Throughout the First Gulf War, we each carried 120 rounds of ammunition, lived under the constant threat of chemical and biological warfare, and received inoculations against Anthrax and the Bubonic Plague. From day one of the war we also had to take Nerve Agent Pre-Treatment tablets, three times daily. Thus, as the Scud missiles attacked – sometimes without warning – we lived with this very real apprehension. During one night we were attacked on five occasions. Nevertheless, how good it was to know the veracity of *Psalm 27 verse 3: "Though a host encamp against me, my heart will not fear, though war arise against me, in spite of this I shall be confident";* and, that my eternal security was not in doubt, no matter what happened to my earthly body. From the commencement of the Gulf War, I was supremely conscious of the constant prayers of God's people, in a way not experienced before, nor since.

During this time, I had the privilege of giving out many Bibles and New Testaments to some of my RAF Regiment colleagues, (and to two of the local population). Later, back in the United Kingdom, I had the joy of leading one of them to the Lord. As part of the RAF Regiment's 50th anniversary celebrations during 1992, I was greatly honoured to be introduced to Her Majesty the Queen.

Throughout my career, I have been privileged to serve on 11 bases, which have included overseas postings in The Netherlands, Germany and Ascension Island (including 2 NATO assignments); I have also been deployed to Hong Kong, Denmark, Norway, Sardinia, Cyprus, Belgium and Alaska, during which I have met some wonderful Christians. God has also blessed me with rich fellowship within the wider SASRA family, which has also included ASR Ivor and May Sherwood.

In the course of the year 2000, although I still had over 13 years to serve in the Royal Air Force, I began to sense that perhaps my service in the RAF was drawing to a close, as God closed various doors. After much prayer I applied to the SASRA Council for the South West of England & South Wales Area Representative post. The SASRA Council endorsed this call, and I'm so thankful to God for the great privilege to serve Him through the unique ministry of SASRA. How good it is to know that He who calls, also equips (*1 Thessalonians 5:24*).

As I reflect back on my 26½ years in the Royal Air Force, it is with profound gratitude to God for the organisation of SASRA. My life has been immeasurably blessed; indeed, the Henagulphs and Hodsons in particular, have made an incalculable impact on my life. My testimony for the past 32 years is this: God **IS** faithful.

Matthew Glass served with the Royal Air Force from October 1974 to May, 2001. He commenced his work with SASRA in May, 2001 as Area Representative for South West England and South Wales.

17

Mr Geoff Hill

I followed my father into the Corps of Royal Engineers, starting as an Army Apprentice at Chepstow in 1958. I was the fifth consecutive member of my family to enter the Corps, looking to the services to complete my education and provide me with a trade. Five years later, in 1963, through the testimony and witness of a SASRA member, and the preaching of a Welsh evangelist, Maynard James, I was led to a saving knowledge of the Lord Jesus Christ at the RSME Chatham.

My wife Pamela, was similarly led to the Lord through the witness and testimony of the SASRA fellowship in Rheindahlen, where she was serving with the WRAF during October 1963. Our joint testimony is that by the grace of God, two young service people, from very different backgrounds, were both saved through the faithful witness and testimony of the SASRA family, to serve the Lord in newness of life.

In the first year of my Christian life, I was much blessed through the ministry of ASR Frank & Vera

Crofts. I used to travel from Herford to Bielefeld to meet with them most weekends. Later, on posting to Rheindahlen, I enjoyed fellowship with John & Joy Findlay. Rheindahlen was of course where I met Pamela.

We were married at Farnham, whilst I was on a Clerk of Works course at the RSME. Through my service years the Lord blessed us with three children, and at the time of writing five grandchildren. All our children and the two marriage partners are born again, and for that we give much thanks to the Lord. Not all are walking in His ways, but their names are written in the Lamb's Book of Life, and we pray they will return to their first love and again worship and serve Him.

Unable before the Lord to accept a Short Service Commission I served to complete my twenty-two years with the colours, and embarked on my civilian career in 1983. By the Lord's good grace I was able to train for, and later practice as an Industrial Safety Consultant for ten years. Keeping only a tenuous link with SASRA we both continued to be active in our local assembly with Covenantors, Sunday School and Youth Club activities. Being invited to join a SASRA prayer conference at Amport House, we were again reminded of the warmth and immediacy of SASRA fellowship, and were encouraged in our hearts to see if we could be active locally. This did not progress beyond finding out that there was already a local representative. The Lord intervened with an invitation through Pat & Jim Eldergill, the South West Area Representatives, to consider the vacant post of South East Area Representative. From the moment of receiving that invitation the Lord gave us no peace until in obedience, after many scriptural challenges and heart searching, some six months later we met with the council and were offered the South East Area Representative's post. But even then I was unsure, and took a further month to meditate on all that had transpired since that first prayer conference. It was a silent month, no helps, challenges or encouragement from the Word of God, or anywhere else for that matter. Then we recognised in our hearts that this was a step of obedience for both of us. The morning we 'surrendered' to His claims on our lives yet again, we read these words which have encouraged and sustained us when the times have been hard. *'Wherefore, seeing we also are compassed about with so great a cloud of witnesses, let us lay aside every weight, and the sin which doth so easily beset us, and let us run with patience the race that is set before us, Looking unto Jesus the author and finisher of our faith ; who, for the joy that was set before him, endured the cross, despising the shame and is set down at the right hand of the throne of God'* (Heb. 12:1-2 KJV).

At the time of writing this testimony I can hardly believe that we are in our thirteenth year of service. At His bidding we happily joined the SASRA family, not really knowing what was before us and not feeling capable or able to do that which was being asked of us. We still feel like beginners, still unsure of many things, but this we have learned in the school of His experience; He is able to keep that which we have committed unto Him, and I am convinced, keep us until that glorious day of His appearing. He has also provided for all our needs, He has enabled me to preach from His Word and tell of His work; He has kept us through thousands of miles of driving, given us an ever expanding family of SASRA supporters, brought us friends we never dreamed of having and joined us in harness with the most special kind of people in all His service, the Scripture Reader and his wife. For this and His many, many blessings, we give Him our thanks, praise and worship.

Geoff Hill served in the Royal Engineers from August 1958 to March, 1983. He commenced his work with SASRA in 1993 as an Area Representative.

18

Lt Col Malcolm Hitchcott MBE

I was born into an Army family and soon began to travel around with my father wherever he was posted. Having attended no less than nine primary schools, I was sent to the Duke of York's Royal Military School in Dover, where I spent five very happy years. After two years at Welbeck College, I joined the Army and went to the Royal Military Academy, Sandhurst, from where I was commissioned into the Royal Electrical and Mechanical Engineers in 1964.

During the initial phase of my Army career the seeds of a 'social' drinking problem were sown. After a false start at the Royal Military College of Science to read for an engineering degree, I completed my engineering studies at Reading. Nonetheless, my drinking problem was still with me. In fact, a motoring accident, in which drink was a factor, nearly cost me my life.

I became qualified as a Chartered Engineer in 1973 and during my subsequent career in the Army, I served in a variety of Staff, Command, Engineering and Instructional appointments. I was serving in

Whitehall at the time of the Falklands War in 1982; I found this exciting and stimulating. Although I had an aptitude for 'desk work', I was never happier than when I was working with soldiers in the training organisation. This I was privileged to be involved with during three separate postings.

One of my desk jobs was in Salisbury, at Headquarters United Kingdom Land Forces, where I worked from 1975 to 1977. It was during a tour just outside Salisbury that I first met Marion, my Brigadier's Personal Secretary. Although we worked closely together during my two year tour, there was never a hint of the romance that was to blossom later on. It was in late 1979 that Marion and I met again; suddenly there was romance in the air and we were married within five months. I certainly found it a change of lifestyle after 36 years of bachelor-hood, to suddenly have a ready made family.

In 1983, I was promoted to Lt Col and posted to Liverpool to take command of a unit. I recall asking what heinous crime I had committed to be sent to Liverpool. Notwithstanding this reaction, I found life in Liverpool enjoyable and challenging. As far as material things were concerned, Marion and I lacked nothing. We had domestic help, a chauffeur driven car, a lovely Army house and two comfortable salaries. Not only did we have virtually everything we wanted, but the prospects for my career in the Army seemed extremely good too. But all this 'success' still did not satisfy – there was something fundamental in my life missing. I tried to fill the void by working long hours and keeping myself busy. I continued the fairly heavy social drinking, but any relief to my emptiness was only ever temporary.

In the summer of 1984, I, along with Marion, was invited to 'Mission England' at Anfield Football Stadium. Both Marion and I had been, and still were, regular church attenders. This was only ever 'something to do', we never knew what God, through Christ, had done for us personally. We accepted the Mission invitation, not because we felt any great need to, but because we were curious to see Billy Graham and hear what he had to say.

That night Billy Graham preached a powerful message. Piece by piece, he stripped away all my smug self righteousness. I realised that before God I was a sinner and there was nothing I could do to atone for my sin. The culmination of his sermon was a quote from the prophet Jeremiah: *'The harvest is past and the summer is ended and we are not saved'*. I was pole-axed, my situation was desperate. Dr Graham then explained how we could obtain God's gracious forgiveness. However, when the appeal was made, I fought against the impulse to respond and won. I had managed to rationalise my feelings: Billy Graham had merely wound up my feelings and was engaging in emotional blackmail. I left the Stadium moved but unresponsive.

Nonetheless, both Marion and I were troubled enough to return to Anfield on the last night of the Mission. As soon as the meeting started, I remember that I was deeply stirred within and knew that the feeling I had experienced on the Wednesday night had been very real, and I knew that I had to commit my life. I looked into Marion's face and immediately sensed that she shared my conviction and we both went forward to make a public commitment to Christ together.

As a result of our commitment our lives changed radically. Suddenly we sensed that we had reached new peaks of fulfilment. For me, certainly, that feeling of inner emptiness had gone. I now felt totally fulfilled and I could see, for the first time, a real purpose to my life. Within a few months, the Lord had made it abundantly clear to us that we were to stay in Liverpool. This meant giving up not only a promising career mid stream, but a large house, chauffeured car, domestic assistance, large salaries, et al. We gladly did it!

After leaving the Army in the Autumn of 1986, I was engaged as the administrator of a local church and the Christian school which it founded. In 1989, I went to Emmanuel Bible College in Birkenhead, studying for two years to obtain a Diploma in Theological and Pastoral Studies. I graduated from the college in the summer of 1991.

Having left the Army in 1986, I had deliberately turned my back completely on the Army. I had had a successful and enjoyable career and I didn't always want to be looking over my shoulder to see what I could have been doing, or what heights I might have scaled if I had stayed in. Imagine my surprise when I was about to go to Emmanuel College and I was virtually offered the job of General Secretary of the Soldiers' and Airmen's Scripture Readers Association.

In the years since I committed my life to Christ and His service, I have never doubted Him, or the course along which He has led me. I can testify to God's faithfulness in undertaking in seemingly impossible situations.

Malcolm Hitchcott was commissioned into the Royal Electrical & Mechanical Engineers in August, 1962. He served as General Secretary with SASRA from September, 1991 until November, 2003. In January, 2004, Lt Col Hitchcott was awarded an MBE in the New Year's Honours list. He concluded his SASRA Ministry in 2003 and returned to Liverpool to take up post as the Practice Manager of a Christian medical practice in the Croxteth district of the city.

19

ASR Bob Hodson

A Scripture Reader! When I started to go to school I could read quite well as a result of attending Sunday School and being taught to read using the Bible as a text book. At the age of eight when a Mission was held in the village where I lived, I answered the Appeal on the final evening and was simply given a 'Covenant Card', which I signed. No other help was given. From then on I considered myself a Christian and later on, if I heard the Gospel, I closed my mind to what I heard, saying to myself, 'But I am already a Christian, I signed that card.' However at that time my name was not in the Lamb's Book of Life.

I was involved with the scouting movement and at the age of seventeen I became a Troop Leader. Being friendly with the Guides Company Leader I began to attend the Village Chapel and after attending for some time, a group of young people conducted a series of three Sunday evening services. They had attended a Methodist Association of Youth Clubs Conference and gave reports at those services. At the second service one shared the testimony of a young

German who had attended, who came to know the Lord while serving on U Boats during the second world war. They were trapped under the sea and although he had had nothing but atheistic teaching, he prayed for their deliverance. They all eventually escaped and he sought out a chaplain in the German Navy who led him to the Lord. After hearing this on the Sunday evening, four days later I had an accident when cycling to work down a steep hill. I was thrown off my cycle, with a large truck hurtling down the road. The driver jammed on his brakes and stopped with the front wheels about eighteen inches from my chest. With the testimony and the accident in my mind and at this time facing up to the sin in my life, when the appeal was given the following Sunday, I still did not make an outward response. I went for a quiet walk. Later that evening I joined two others who were being counselled and, as a repentant sinner, I trusted the Lord for forgiveness of all my sins, accepting God's promise in *John 1:9*. This was the day Prince Charles was born.

I was called up to do my National Service at the age of twenty-one when I had completed an engineering apprenticeship. After receiving my call up papers and before reporting, Scripture Reader Ernest Wigg came to a church in Lincoln where I was attending and I spoke with him. I told him that I was to be posted to Aldershot. As he visited the camp he promised to look me up.

On my second night he came into the room of about twenty men with my sergeant and called out loud for me. The Lord's colours were therefore nailed firmly to the mast. This gave me real opportunities for witness. Some of these same men were posted with me for further training. During my service, thirteen months of which were spent in five different training units, I had fellowship and was blessed through the ministry of Scripture Readers Wigg, Purslow, Baxter and occasionally others. On posting to Osnabrück, Germany, when ASR Brockies arrived he often spent his day off with me for fellowship.

On leaving the Army, the Lord clearly called me to study at Lebanon Missionary Bible College and whilst there, I visited the Depot of the Kings Own Scottish Borderers to conduct a Bible Study established by two ladies who ran a Mission in the town, Berwick upon Tweed. The Lord blessed the work there and I, realising the opportunities, applied to be appointed as a part-time Scripture Reader. I was accepted in 1954 and continued whilst in college until 1956. Having been informed that, as I had only served for two years in the Army, I would not qualify for the appointment as a full time Reader, I went to help at the Sandes Soldiers' Homes for six months. After this time I returned to my home, went back to the firm where I had done my apprenticeship, and worked as a part-time Scripture Reader. I visited the two barracks in Lincoln and the RAF Hospital at Nocton Hall. I also had opportunities on some of the RAF stations in the area.

At the end of 1958 I was offered the appointment as a full time Reader and, in 1959 went out to Aden. I was really blessed not only in the work but also through fellowship with missionaries. This was to continue later when I moved on to Hong Kong and Singapore. These servants of God were a real blessing to me. It was whilst working in Aden that I met and married my wife Barbara. We have served the Lord in many places and have now retired from the work.

ASR Bob Hodson served in the Royal Army Service Corps and the Royal Engineers from October, 1950 to October, 1952. His work as a part-time Scripture Reader began in 1954 and in 1958, he was appointed a full-time Reader. He retired as a full time Reader in 1995, but continued part-time until August, 1999.

20

ASR John Holden

I was brought up in a Methodist family. My Dad was a lay preacher and a Sunday School teacher. As children, we had to go to chapel in the mornings, Sunday School in the afternoons and accompany Dad on his preaching engagements. You can imagine that there was great delight with us kids, when my Dad fell out with the church and we did not have to go any longer. As a result, I was able to join my mates out on the streets over the whole weekend. I had just reached the age of fifteen and soon got into trouble with the law and at school, which led to me being asked to leave.

In 1970, I joined the Army as a junior bandsman at Whittington Barracks in Lichfield. I soon was in a great deal of trouble, mainly for fighting and drinking offences. After two and a half years, I was posted to the Royal Military School of Music at Kneller Hall, Twickenham.

It was while I was at Kneller Hall, that I started to become interested in Christianity. It came about by an encounter with a man called Paul Martin, who was a committed Christian and lived in a room opposite to me. One evening near the end of the month, when I had no money left, I was in my room on my own, feeling pretty low at the time. Paul came in and we began to talk about music and even started to play a few duets together. I do not know to this day how we came round to talking about Christ and salvation but we did. I began to realise that something was missing from my life. I had been trying to fill it with drink and sex but the Lord's hand was upon me and he was not going to let go.

I looked into Christianity for the next six months or so. I looked at Christians I knew and the church to which I had started to go. One evening Paul said something to me that hit me for six. He just mentioned that I was looking at Christianity from the outside inwards.

On the evening of March 4th 1973, I just could not get to sleep. I kept on thinking about sin and where this would lead me and that I did not need to go there. The Lord was speaking to me and I realised I needed to do something about my condition. I went out onto the sports ground, knelt down and began to ask the Lord Jesus Christ to forgive me for all my sin. At this point I began to cry. (I had been told by my Dad when I was ten, that big boys do not cry.) Here I was, kneeling in the middle of the sports ground and crying like a baby, as the Lord began His work of Salvation in New Birth. I went back to bed at 2 o'clock on the 5th March. I knew that I was a new creation. Paul saw me the next day and I told him what had happened in the early hours of the morning. The other men in my barrack room saw a great change in my life style. I praise the Lord for the way He has kept His hand on my life and for leading me into the work of SASRA, in order that I might lead others to Him.

To the Lord be all the glory!

John Holden joined the Staffordshire Regiment in April, 1970 and served in the Regular Army until September, 1984. He commenced his work with SASRA in April, 1985.

21

TSR Neil Innes

I was brought up in a crofting community in the Scottish Highlands, which was an idyllic experience. Idyllic indeed; no running water came from our taps, for there were no taps. One of my earliest chores was to draw buckets of water from the well! No supermarkets dominated our shopping, there wasn't even a corner shop from which to buy! No electricity lit up our evenings, oil lamps were the order of the night! No leisure centre or swimming pool was available to occupy our spare time, we spent our evenings reading books or playing table games. Our link with the outside world came through the use of a small battery operated radio into which we tuned for the news bulletin morning and evening. Television wasn't thought of! Most significantly of all, our days both began and ended with a reading from the Bible.

I was educated in the county of Ross-shire at Lochussie and Maryburgh primary schools. My secondary education took place at Dingwall Academy. It was here I was introduced to Scripture Union and to the practice of reading for oneself, a daily portion of holy Scripture. It was also at this time that I came into contact with an organisation called SASRA, The Soldiers' & Airmen's Scripture Readers Association, through the then Scottish Representative of SASRA, Robert Stephen.

Reference has already been made to the daily practice of family worship in the home, at which time a metrical Psalm would be read and sung, a portion of Scripture read and prayer offered. In addition, regular attendance at church was something that was required and expected. Each week, I would regularly walk at least sixteen miles in order to sit under the preaching of the Gospel and also attended Sunday School. At the time, I found all this very tedious. There was no bright hymn or chorus singing in our church, we sang only from the metrical Psalms. No organ or piano accompanied the praise. This was the task of the Presenter or Song Leader. The address or sermon lasted a minimum of forty five minutes. Sermonettes were unheard of!

As I now record something of the crisis experience that finally brought me to faith in Christ, it is with the realisation that all that had gone before was part of God's gracious plan to make Himself real to me. On the face of it, I led a fairly upright life as a youngster, when I was found in the company of Christians more frequently than most of my age. Indeed, there might have been many times because of the outward veneer that I would have passed as a Christian. That was the outward appearance, inwardly, I was in a mess. Deceit, dishonesty, unbelief, envy, jealousy, greed, to mention but a few of the characteristics of the human heart, were rife in my life. I had religion but I did not have Jesus Christ. As God the Holy Spirit drew me into a living relationship with Christ, He used all I had heard in the past and finally, the gift of the Evangelist. In 1954 a Godly minister of the Free Church of Scotland the late Rev W R MacKay who came to Strathpeffer to conduct a week of evangelistic meetings, I was invited to attend by a Godly aunt of my mother. On the Wednesday evening, I left the church in a state of turmoil. I do not recall the text preached on that occasion but suddenly I sensed the awesomeness of God's Presence and the reality of my guilt. I spent a sleepless night as I tossed and turned. The battle for my soul was on! The enemy was real as he sowed seeds of unbelief and questions of doubt. Morning came! At that time I was employed as an engineer's assistant on the Hydro Electric Schemes in Wester Ross. I thought, 'A good hard day's work will sort this lot out.' It didn't! Thursday night and Friday night were spent in the same way as God the Holy Spirit convicted me of sin. At 5a.m. on Saturday morning, I opened the attic window of my bedroom and looked out on a beautiful sunrise. I remembered the Psalmist's words in *Psalm 19:1, 'The heavens declare the Glory of God; and the skies proclaim the work of His hands.'*

Returning to the evangelistic meetings on Saturday night, I was to hear Mr MacKay preach from *Revelation 22:17, 'The Spirit and the bride say, Come! and let him who hears say, Come! Whoever is thirsty, let him come; and whoever wishes, let him take the free gift of the water of life.'*

Also in the service four young men gave their

testimonies. All spoke of the reality of Christ having replaced religion in their experience. During the preaching that evening God met with me in a very real way and I began to feel a sense of peace, as the clouds of conviction were blown away by the wind of the Spirit. I left the church sensing the peace of God in my soul. As I journeyed home that evening, I asked myself the question, 'How do I know this is real?' Mr MacKay had pointed out to me that *we are saved by Grace through Faith,'* not by feelings. I knew it was real when later that evening the Bible was opened and read. The book that had been so dead and boring became to me the living Word of God.

Following a missionary meeting in 1955, I was called to the work of an Evangelist. Responding to the challenge of God's Word and His Spirit, I reasoned with God as I cycled home. I could cycle no further. Abandoning my cycle at the roadside, I sat down on a rock in the grass verge and surrendered my life to Christ for service. Then, thumbing through my Bible before restarting my journey home, God spoke to me so clearly from *2 Timothy 4:2,5. 'Preach the Word; be prepared in season and out of season; correct, rebuke and encourage – with great patience and careful instruction. ...But you, keep your head in all situations, endure hardship, do the work of an evangelist, discharge all the duties of your ministry.'*

Nine years later having served as a regular soldier in the RAMC, during which time I met Barbara Fraser, who was soon to become my wife. Within the first year of our marriage, the Lord revealed to us the mission field to which God had called me was not some far flung place across the universe but, the Armed Forces of our own nation. Barbara had felt called to serve the Lord, perhaps in the Far East or China. (Her testimony reveals how this was fulfilled.) In a wonderful way however, the Lord confirmed the call into SASRA. While on duty at my final unit in Rhyl, North Wales late one night, God spoke to me from the call of Abraham (*Gen. 12*) and confirmed His call into the work of SASRA. You can imagine my thrill and amazement when I returned home the next day to find Barbara's Bible lying open in our bedroom at *Genesis 12*. How good God is! It is essential to have the partner of God's choosing and if called to embark on Christian service for the Lord, that your partner shares that call. We applied to SASRA and were accepted to work full time as a husband and wife team from 1st July, 1965.

After my six month training period in Germany, Catterick, and RAF Lyneham we were posted to Edinburgh, where we served until October 1972. This was followed by a tour in Bielefeld, Germany until 1976, from where we returned to the UK for a short posting in Colchester, Essex, prior to taking over responsibility for Scotland, the Isle of Man and English Border Counties as Area Representative, with a travelling role as a Scripture Reader. We thank God for all his faithfulness over those many years during which we have known mountain top and valley experiences but, have proved again and again, His unfailing love and the truth of His Word *'I will never leave thee, nor forsake thee.' Hebrews 13:5.*

Neil Innes served in the Royal Army Medical Corps

from June, 1956 to June, 1965. He began his ministry as a full time Scripture Reader on 1st July, 1965 and subsequently became Area Representative for Scotland, with a Travelling Scripture Reader role on 1ˢᵗ June, 1977. Neil retired from full time work with SASRA on 31st December, 2005.

This testimony has been abridged and extracted from 'IS THAT YOUR VOICE LORD?' published by Christian Focus Publications 1995.

22

Mrs Barbara Innes

Nestling deep in the heart of the Cumbrian countryside, overshadowed by the Pennine Hills and indeed, in the centre of the Pennine Way, lies the tiny village of Garrigill, five miles from Alston, at the time the highest market town in the Pennines. It was to a terraced house on the edge of the village green, that the family who were living there, had been evacuated from Bognor Regis in Sussex during the second world war. Douglas and Fanny Smith, who herself had been borne and brought up in the nearby village of Haltwhistle, had found a safe haven in which to reside during those difficult years, taking with them their eldest daughter Nancy and her younger sister Elsie. The latter was married to Archibald Fraser, who, during this period was serving as a Corporal in the Royal Army Service Corps.

On 23rd May, 1943, Elsie gave birth to her second daughter, Barbara Mathieson Fraser. Thus I had begun my earthly journey. My Grandparents and their two daughters attended one of the two Methodist Churches in the village and my sister Ruth and I were taken into the church environment from the very earliest childhood. This continued when we were repatriated to Bognor at the end of the war and, indeed, I can never remember a time when I was not influenced by the Christian message through my Aunt taking me to Sunday School each Sunday and as I grew older, by the influence of being given Christian story books and missionary stories to read. My mother presided over bedtime prayers and we made a rota of who of the three of us, (we had by this time been joined by our younger brother Ian), would say grace at each meal.

Just prior to my eighth birthday, we moved house from Bognor to Bishopbriggs on the outskirts of Glasgow. Life there was very different in many ways. I missed my friends and in particular, a girl called Joyce, who had taken me to school on my first day. She lived across the road from us with her two younger brothers and parents, committed Christians whose prayers have followed me all my life. No doubt as a result of these prayers, on arrival in Bishopbriggs, I was to come under the godly influence of my Primary School Teacher Miss M MacIver, who not only taught my brother and I but also, many years later, our daughter Ruth and son Jonathan.

I had always loved listening to my aunt, who was a concert pianist, playing the piano and, now I became keen to learn to play the piano for myself. By the time I was in my early teens, I was teaching in the Sunday School and playing the piano for the Girls Guildry in the Church of Scotland which we were now attending.

Despite all these years of exposure to the Christian

message, it wasn't until I had reached the age of
fifteen, on 7th March, 1959 in fact, that I attended
a service in St George's Tron Parish Church in
Glasgow, which was to be instrumental in changing
my life and indeed my eternal destiny. I had been
invited there by my school friend Marjory King.
Following on from Dr Billy Graham's Crusade in
the Kelvin Hall, Glasgow in 1955, the late Rev Tom
Allan had continued running monthly meetings
or rallies, known as the 'Tell Scotland' Rallies, in
the Tron Church in the heart of that great city of
Glasgow. As Mr Allan faithfully preached the Gospel
that night and, Sir David McNee sang the solo, *'Why
did they nail Him to Calvary's tree,'* I heard with
understanding, for the first time, that I was a sinner
and that the Lord Jesus Christ loved me so much
that He had gone all the way to Calvary in order
to pay the price for my sin and, had I been the only
person in the world, He would still have died for
me. As I observed Rev Tom Allan singing the words
of the hymn, *'Dear Saviour Thou art mine'* and the
words of the chorus, *'Mine, mine, mine, I know Thou
art mine,'* I realised he had an assurance which I
didn't possess and so, as the choir sang, *'Just as I
am and waiting not to rid my soul of one dark blot,
to Thee whose blood can cleanse each spot, O Lamb of
God, I come.'* I went forward to make my personal
commitment to Jesus Christ.

I made mention earlier in this testimony, that
I had been given missionary stories to read in my
formative years and, in a strange way I guess, I had
sensed from that time, that I should one day go to
the mission field. Where, I was never quite sure but,

my interest had always been focused on China or the Far East. After completing my education in Whitehill Secondary School in Glasgow, I spent a number of months doing nursing training but, soon sensing that this was not for me, I left and began a secretarial course. On completion of my secretarial diploma, I obtained employment in the Public Relations Department of the 52 Lowland District of the Army in Scotland. Soon I noticed a young Sgt visiting the office. Sometimes he wore civilian clothes and in his lapel a badge which I had never seen before. At this time, I also worked on a Saturday in Pickering & Inglis Book Shop. One morning, just after the shop had opened, in walked the Sgt. I introduced myself to him and asked about the badge he was wearing. This was my first introduction to a SASRA badge, for Neil Innes, as I discovered him to be, was indeed a committed Christian and a SASRA member.

We began seeing one another and witnessing together in an open air team on a Saturday night in Dalhousie Street/Sauchiehall Street, Glasgow. As our relationship continued, I was faced with a dilemma. Was my developing friendship with Neil, which looked increasingly like becoming permanent, really of the Lord? How could it be the Lord's Will for me to consider marriage with someone who was in the Forces, when I still felt very strongly about the mission field.

About this time I attended a ladies' missionary meeting where Mrs Lyn Stanford had spoken. That night all those years of sensing a call to the mission field suddenly came into sharp focus and I knew, without a doubt, that I had to respond to the call of the great commission. Now, the battle was on! We had always sought to put the Lord first in our relationship so, how could the Lord allow me to find myself in this situation. I couldn't understand! I told Neil I would have to very seriously consider whether I could continue to see him and would need time to pray about it!

The following Friday evening, I attended with my Bible Class, a meeting in Porch Hall Assembly in Glasgow. That night, like a bolt out of the blue, the Lord spoke to me so clearly through the verse of Scripture which was ministered on in *John 13:35* *'By this shall all men know that ye are my disciples, if ye have love one towards another.'* I could scarcely believe it, much less understand how it could work out. I just had to trust and obey.

We were married on 18th August, 1964 and I joined Neil in his last unit before demob from the Army. Although Neil had been approached and asked to take up one of the first RAMC Commissions in the Army, he like me, had felt called to full time Christian Service. Neil takes up the story in his testimony, when he recounts how the Lord spoke to both of us very clearly through the call of Abraham from *Genesis 12* and confirmed our call into the work of SASRA. Again I thought, 'Lord, that's not China and neither is it the Far East' but still I knew it was right and the next step to take.

In July, 1965, our ministry with SASRA, The Soldiers and Airmen's Scripture Readers Association, began and, in January, 1966, we took up our first appointment after Neil's period of training, as the Garrison Scripture Reader in Edinburgh. It was in this Garrison two years later, that the Lord was to bring into focus that call to the Far East when together, we launched the SASRA outreach ministry at the Edinburgh Military Tattoo. On that occasion, we experienced our first opportunity of reaching out with the Gospel to the Gurkha soldiers from the land of Nepal. In particular, I recall with great joy, the occasion in our home at Swanston Gardens when we entertained for a curry lunch, in excess of thirty Gurkhas who had shown a real interest in Christianity. Thus began a ministry that has continued over these thirty plus years. What a joy it is to know that some of these little men and their wives have been brought to faith in the Lord Jesus Christ through the impact of the Word of God which we have placed in their hands.

Finally, I want to record my gratitude to God for His faithfulness to us as a family and to myself, as an individual. He has enabled me to cope with many difficult situations over the years. In recent times, I have proved His faithfulness again and again as I have coped with breast cancer and more recently with a recurrence. How thankful I am that He has given us His word and that His promises are sure. He has taught me to understand in some small way the truth of *1 Thessalonians 5:18 'In everything give thanks'* and in my most recent experiences, a word that has become exceedingly precious is *Isaiah 41:10 'Fear thou not: for I am with thee: be not dismayed; for I am thy God: I will strengthen thee; yea, I will help thee; yea I will uphold thee with the right hand of my righteousness.'*

The Lord has blessed us with four children, Rachel, Ruth, Jonathan and Timothy all of whom are married. We have eight grandchildren, Paul & Hannah, Benjamin & Charlotte, Abigail & Rebekah, Claire & Ainsley Joy.

23

Lt Col Ann Kerr ARRC

It was during my first tour of Hong Kong in 1975, that I came to know Jesus Christ as my personal Saviour. This came as a quiet realisation of a faith that I had practised from early childhood. Therefore to tell the whole story I return to my formative years.

For the benefit of those who may not know me, my roots are in Northern Ireland. At a very early age, as one of five children with a Christian mother. I remember being taken to Sunday School each Sunday morning. In the afternoon I would attend the children's church service of the Parish, accompanied by my mother. Throughout my life I never doubted the existence of God, the truth of the Bible or of Jesus Christ.

I was brought up in the Church of Ireland, baptised and confirmed and in my youth, was a member of the choir and actively involved in church activities. In adult life, I continued as a regular churchgoer, never realising that there was anything else required of me. I was religious and therefore a Christian!

Three years into my service career I went along

to St Andrew's Church, Nathan Road, Hong Kong and realised that there was something missing from my Christian faith. The church services were so different from what I had been accustomed to, with a teaching ministry which opened the Scriptures to reveal that, with all the Bible teaching and instruction I had previously received, I had never consciously considered that I needed to ask God's forgiveness for my sins and to accept Him into my life. Yes, I believed in Jesus Christ as the Son of God, that He had died on the cross. Yes, that He had risen and had ascended into heaven. All of this I had been taught as a child, but I never gave much thought beyond the cross and that I needed to be saved. Also during my early days at St Andrew's I came to know other service Christians and the joy and presence of Christ in their lives was something I longed for. By now I knew what I had to do. So, one Sunday, in the quiet of my bedroom in the Officers' Mess, I knelt by the side of my bed and asked God to forgive my sins and accepted Christ as my Saviour.

Following on from this I enjoyed some wonderful fellowship. I can especially remember going along to the Billy Graham Crusade with a Christian nursing colleague. This was the first time I had been in such a gathering of people. Praising God in the Open Air was completely new to me. Within, I wanted to have a greater knowledge and understanding of God's Word and I recall going in search of a Christian book shop and purchasing the simplest of books to explain basic Christianity. I started to read the Bible daily with the aid of Scripture Union notes. I was like a child again returning to the very basics of learning, and indeed I had much to learn. I also attended Bible Fellowship meetings in the home of Captain Tim Symonds and his wife Zinnia, where I received a warm and loving welcome. Before I knew it 1975 was gone, I was into 1976 and packing to return to the United Kingdom.

Posted to Catterick, I wanted to be certain that I would continue to grow as a Christian and so I joined the Officers Christian Union (OCU) to help encourage me in my faith through the availability of Christian material and the likelihood of meeting other OCU members. Soon after arriving at my new unit, I met up with an RAF friend of mine, who had also become a Christian. We were able to share fellowship and attend a Bible Study group together.

Having accepted Christ as my Saviour in 1975, the one thing I had omitted to do, was to make a public confession of faith and it was not until 1977 at a Dales Bible Week Convention, that I responded to an appeal by the speaker to do just that, and later that week I was baptised by total immersion, as an open witness of my faith.

I admit to having experienced spiritual lows throughout my Christian walk. Never was this always obvious to anyone else, although God knew. I have kept no diary, but such down periods have taken place during tours of duty where fellowship has been lacking; in situations of tiredness following long working hours and in-discipline in prayer and Bible study. In all these situations when I would eventually realise I could not go it alone and then hand myself completely into the Lord's hands. With Him in control I would always be lifted out of the shadows and refilled with strength through God's grace. Thank God for His faithfulness.

Over many years and postings, I have valued hospitality and fellowship in the homes of Scripture Readers and OCU members. Although associated with SASRA since the late 70s, amazingly, it was not until 1991 when I came to know the late Charles Witts and his wife Edna, that Charles encouraged me to join SASRA. I considered that having membership of OCU was sufficient! Charles convinced me of the importance to belong to both. This was wise counsel. Throughout my career I have made a point of supporting the local Garrison Church, having once heard an OCU member say ' Support your Army Chaplain'.

I retired from the QARANC mid 1996 as part of reorganisation of the Armed Forces and spent the next four years living in Farnham, Surrey, but continuing to worship at the Royal Garrison Church of all Saints, Aldershot, where I took an active role in the church. Being so settled in my surroundings and all that I was involved with, I never expected to move. However, illness and other family circumstances caused me to re-evaluate where I was living and so, after much thought and prayer I felt the Lord telling me to return to Northern Ireland. Moving in July 2000 it sometimes seems to me that I have completed a circle by returning to my roots! While attending the local parish church, I have made some wonderful friends with a love of the Lord. I continue as a SASRA Council Member and am also pleased to form part of the Northern Ireland SASRA support group. *"To God be the glory great things He has done."*

Ann Kerr was commissioned into the QARANC in October, 1968. She joined the SASRA Council in April, 1996.

24

The late ASR Jim Kirk

I was brought up in the heart of the country and went very little to Sunday school as it was considered too far to walk. Both school and Sunday school were some three miles distant and of course in those days, there was no public transport. The consequence was that I grew up in total ignorance of the Word of God and did not know one single Bible story.

Immediately after leaving school, I went to church on occasions but soon discontinued the practice, as I felt too much of a hypocrite and, as far as I could judge, benefited nothing from church going. It was more of a sentence each Sunday and sermons bored me to tears. I could only conclude that there was nothing in the Christian faith to meet the needs of a young life or satisfy the heart. Nevertheless, during these difficult years as a teenager, I had a desire to be a true Christian. I did not know how until one day I heard an ex RSM of the Royal Scots preach Christ in the open air at the mound in Edinburgh. He had a great deal more back bone than jaw bone and I was attracted more by his character, as he seemed to have something in his life that very few men possessed. Through this remarkable man, I heard the Gospel that Jesus Christ had died for me personally and risen again and, this made it possible for me to be born again and be saved from sin. From the moment I embraced the Lord Jesus as my personal Saviour, I began to experience an inward change. It was a genuinely real experience which I saw grow in me day by day and, a change which others could see also.

The first member of the body to display the work of grace in my heart was the tongue. The Word of God says, *'The tongue can no man tame,'* but there is One who can take the tongue and remove the poison. I acquired a hunger for God's Holy Word I never knew before. The desire and the ability to pray was also given to me. I saw for the first time that the Bible is the Word of God. I found, too, that the Lord Jesus brought into my life a joy and peace I never knew before. The desire for strong drink was taken away, as was the cigarette, the cinema and the theatre.

An ex-Army man introduced me to Carrubbers Mission where I attended a Bible Study which was also led by an ex-soldier. I discovered some of the gifts that God had given me as I joined the Open Air Witness Team at the Mission. At this time, I worked in a building firm and through a colleague at work, I met May MacLean, who was later to become my wife. I served for five years in the Royal Navy, completing two tours of duty in the Mediterranean. Here I experienced the traumas and rigors of war, learning something of the brevity of life and the stewardship which we have as Christians of the Gospel message.

As a young Christian in the Forces, He enabled me by His grace to maintain a bed side witness and to overcome the fear of man. It is a most wonderful thing to be lifted out of a nominal Christianity and translated into a living union with Christ in death and resurrection, by the power of the Holy Spirit and, also into a personal relationship with a risen Lord and soon coming King. Following the end of the war in 1945, May and I were married and later, the Lord blessed us with two children, Kathleen and Howard.

In May, 1946, we entered the Lord's work through SASRA and discovered the privilege of working as an Army Scripture Reader among young men in H M Forces, in barrack rooms, guardrooms and hospital wards. It has been my greatest joy to see many Servicemen of different nationalities and denominations, good living men and bad, come to experience the same radical change which 'new birth' brings through the Cross to those who truly believe.'

One of the highlights of our ministry began in 1962, when a Battalion of Gurkha soldiers were located in Tidworth, Hampshire, where I was the resident Scripture Reader. Although not permitted by the authorities to visit the Gurkhas, the SASRA bungalow was located on the edge of the camp and through a remarkable set of circumstances, we became acquainted with a Corporal from the Gurkha Transport Regiment, who was a Christian. This contact began twelve months of constant daily outreach to them. The SASRA bungalow in Tidworth was to many of these lads a real home from home, sometimes from early morning to late at night. When one Gurkha told another that he had made the bungalow his home, the reply was, 'I shall make it my home too,' and he certainly did. They made use of the drawers for their belongings, decorated the walls with pictures, and cooked Nepali curries in the kitchen. These had to be eaten in real Nepali style, i.e. squatting on the floor owing to a lack of seating accommodation. We ourselves developed a real taste for the curries and thoroughly enjoyed having these men in our home at all times.

Several hundred of the Gurkha soldiers with their families passed the bungalow every Saturday and Sunday on their way to the cinema and, as the Nepalese like singing, Gurkhali hymns were played on the tape recorder with the windows wide open. Many stood on the road outside and listened to the messages in song, others came in to hear these hymns. In this way opportunities were provided for personal talks and the distribution of portions of Holy Scripture. I think of one man who came here regularly and listened to the Gospel message, but never seemed moved or affected in any way. He was repatriated to the Far East owing to a domestic problem. Many months later, I received a letter from him to say he had come to the Saviour, as Jesus had answered all his prayers and solved his domestic problems. *'Cast thy bread upon the waters for thou shalt find it after many days.'*

Jim Kirk served as a full time Scripture Reader with SASRA from 1946 until 1976. He was called home to be with the Lord on 7th May, 1994. His wife May (until her death on 15th September, 2005) maintained her interest in Forces' evangelism acting as the leader of the Armed Forces' Christian Union Associates Prayer Group in Edinburgh and was a regular attender at the monthly SASRA Prayer Meeting.

H.M. The Queen Patron of SASRA
and Maj Gen. Sir Lawrence New

ASR Meg Atkinson

ASR Bob & Ruth Barbour

Steven & Lynda Carter

ASR Sally Clarke

ASR Bob &
Jean Clayton

Gen Sir Richard Dannatt

Brig W I C Dobbie

ASR Jim & Debbie Downie
with Kirsten & Cêara

ASR Berenice Ducker

ASR John & Doreen Dunbar

Maj Gen Ian & Janie Durie

Mr Jim & Pat Eldergill

ASR Bob & Anne Elliot

ASR Lily Frampton

ASR David &
Joan Gibson

Mr Matthew Glass

Mr Geoff & Pam Hill

Lt Col Malcolm & Marion Hitchcott

ASR Bob & Barbara Hodson

ASR John &
Pauline Holden

TSR Neil &
Barbara Innes

Lt Col Ann Kerr

The late ASR Jim & May Kirk

Maj Iain Alasdair &
Ella Macdonald

ASR John & Sandra
McIllmurray

ASR Mel & Barbara Moodie

ASR Jim & Gertie Moore

ASR Ernest & Margaret Paddon

ASR Lee & Debbie Philipson

ASR Sinclair & Valerie Quinn

ASR Mark &
Jeanette Reynolds

ASR John &
Audrey Rowlands

Maj Philip &
Elizabeth Shannon

ASR Ivor &
May Sherwood

ASR Paul &
Gillian Somerville

ASR Alastair &
Pat Stewart

ASR William & Tulsi Wade

ASR Nick & Dolly Wilson

Sqn Ldr Colin Woodland

ASR Bill & Pat Woolfall

ASR Derek & Barbara Yarwood

25
Major Iain A MacDonald

I had the privilege of being brought up in a Christian home where family worship was held morning and evening. I attended church twice every Lord's Day and was fortunate enough to hear some of the greatest Christian men in deep discussion and debate in my family home. My father was totally disabled with rheumatoid arthritis, and often in great pain, which he bore with great fortitude. He was a shinning example as a Christian and greatly respected by all.

By the age of sixteen I was similar to the prodigal son, desperately wanting to get away from the Christian restraints of home. The only way I could see open to me was to leave Lewis and join the Army, a career I had always wanted to follow. After much debate and heart searching on the part of my parents they reluctantly allowed me to join the army as a boy soldier at the Junior Tradesmen's Regiment Troon where I first came in contact with SASRA.

In 1968 I was posted to the Persian Gulf for nine months. During that time there had been a revival on the Island of Lewis affecting many of my friends in the village of Callanish on the West coast of the Island. Most of the young men and many women were converted.

Christians from all over the Island were drawn to house meetings, which were being held in homes virtually every night of the week. During my time in the Gulf, I received a birthday card from a close friend. In the card was part of his testimony, ending with the words, "I know that if you were honest with yourself, you would love more than anything in the world that you would be saved." I remember weeping bitterly in my desert tent knowing in my heart that that was my greatest desire.

When I came back from the Gulf, we were given six weeks leave which I spent at home in Lewis. During the first four weeks I kept as far away from my former friends as was possible. I could not see how anyone could be a Christian in the army. I had met a girl since coming home and we saw each other regularly. One evening towards the end of my holiday I had a date with her, but as had been my custom, I would borrow my mother's car and drive around the town first. Whilst driving in town my friend who had sent the birthday card stopped me and asked me if I could give himself and some friends a lift to the village of Callanish to a house meeting. I was only too pleased, being only about sixteen miles from Stornoway, which would give me plenty of time to return to town for my date. Five young people piled into my mother's small Morris Minor. On arrival the lady who owned the house met us and persuaded me to join the others. I was amazed. The house was full mainly with young people. The meeting went on past midnight.

The meeting made a great impression upon me. So much so that when I returned to my unit two days later, I told my friends that I would no longer be going out on the town with them. That statement was made in early afternoon, by eight in the evening I was out with them. My conscience had been awakened. I no longer felt comfortable in their company, sadly for the next four months my reaction was to rebel even more to try and drown my awakened conscience. I was under conviction of sin.

During this time my father's health deteriorated and I was called home. I was given a week's compassionate leave. On Sunday evening whilst my mother and sister were in church, my father asked me to read to him, but little did I realize at the time that he was asking me to read portions of scripture that were more relevant to my situation than his. I could feel the tears welling up in my eyes but trying hard not to show it.

I returned to my unit the next day to go straight on exercise. During the exercise every free moment was spent reading the bible and a Christian book I had been given, often weeping over the words I was reading. Halfway through the exercise the Padre came to inform me that my father had passed away.

When I went home to Lewis, as is the custom, worship was held in the home of the bereaved for a number of nights. On my first night home, I remember listening to Rev D Gilles praying and found myself agreeing with all that he was saying. After worship I went up the stairs into my room knowing that the Lord had changed my life. I remember going on my knees and feeling a wonderful peace filling my soul. I recall praying that God would use me for his own glory.

I thought then that I would have to leave the

army but I soon found that that was not his will for me. He soon showed me that I was in the place of his appointment. After coming to Inverness in 1991 from Munster in Germany, I was elected an elder in Greyfriars Free Church and as a presbytery elder I was elected to the Scottish council of the LDOS. One of the committee suggested that I should give prayerful consideration to the position of Scottish secretary. I gave it little thought initially. I was very happy doing my work and still had six years to serve. As time went on I felt convinced that the Lord was calling me into the work. When I telephoned the chairman to inform him of my decision he said that he had been expecting my call. This was a great encouragement to me. I had now been in the work four years and for some time I had felt that the Lord was directing me in a different path.

During the second Gulf War, I was given a great burden for the soldiers serving in the Gulf and in Afghanistan. I shared this burden with my wife who also had a burden for the soldiers and their wives. After much thought and prayer I felt that my work with LDOS was coming to a close. This was confirmed by a letter received by a Christian brother who suggested I should consider coming into the work of SASRA as the Scottish Representative. After much prayer and consultation with Christian brethren in the church, I felt that the Lord was calling me into the work. My prayer is that the Lord will open many doors for the furtherance of the Gospel in our forces and enable me to make the Christian public more aware of the need of prayer for them in these days of uncertainty due to the terrorist threat.

The Lord has left us in no doubt of the part prayer has to play in missionary enterprise. He clearly placed it on a prayer basis in the memorable words:

"The harvest truly is plenteous but the labourers are few. Pray ye therefore the Lord of the harvest and he will send forth labourers into his harvest."

Iain MacDonald joined the Army in September, 1966 as a junior soldier. In April, 1968 he joined the 1st Bn Queens Own Highlanders in Berlin. Iain was commissioned in November, 1988 and retired from the Army in the rank of Major on 31st December, 2000. He is married to Ella and they have three grown up daughters. Iain became Area Representative of Scotland, the Isle of Man and the Northern English Border Counties on 1st January, 2006.

26

ASR John McIllmurray

I grew up in a regimental home, well disciplined and provided for and yet very sad. Much strife existed between my parents ending often in violence. I remember at the age of fourteen vowing to myself that I would never be like my Dad and I would leave home as soon as possible. I even remember asking God to help me live a life that would please Him or words to that effect, although all I knew about Him was that He turned up for Remembrance Day Parades.

Joining the Army at the age of sixteen was like the 'Great Escape'. I was determined to do well and aided by athletic attributes, I did just that. Joining my unit in Hong Kong spelt riotous living. This was fine by me. After all, didn't someone, somewhere owe me some happiness? As a matter of fact, I cannot exactly remember being happy. Sick, yes and with less money in the bank but not happy! I guess before I thought about it for too long, I was drinking again and forgot all about it.

The 'Status Quo 'of my life however, took a

sudden and dramatic turn on 4th February, 1989. My fitness which had been my pride and joy and promised promotion, was taken out of the picture, as I lay on a hospital bed in intense pain from a hill run. I was to find out five years later, that I had ruptured a disk. The news became worse when my Platoon Commander came two days later, to tell me that my Dad was on the telephone. Broken in body and now in spirit, I crawled back to the ward. My only sister was dead and my whole existence crumpled into nothingness. It was in this state of emptiness, soothed slightly by alcohol abuse, that in July 1990, I met with the Scripture Reader in Catterick where my unit was now located. He was invited into our four man room and chatted with us. I requested a Bible, having never read or owned one in my life. An invitation to church and to his home followed. The Reader never had to explain what the Bible said about sin. For five months I strove to become a better person to please God.

On the night of Christmas Eve 1990 I broke. On my knees by my bed I sobbed as I asked Jesus to take the reigns of this runaway, heading for destruction, thanking Him for dying for me. I committed my life to Him and asked Him to take my body and use it as He willed. After all, it had not fared too well under it's previous ownership. All was new! Hatred of my father was gone, love filled the parts that Heineken Beer had failed to reach and for the first time in my life, I was happy. The medical discharge came and even in the midst of an uncertain future, there was hope. I ended up in Bible College and was married at the end of my second year to Sandra, who had been a City Missionary in Newcastle. We felt called to the work of evangelism and applied to SASRA. The Council accepted us for a full time appointment in September, 1994.

John McIllmurray served in the Duke of Edinburgh's Royal Regiment from August, 1987 to December, 1991. He began his work with SASRA as a Scripture Reader in September, 1994. Sadly John resigned from SASRA on health grounds in January, 2006.

27

ASR Mel Moodie

I was born and brought up in Edinburgh and lived in quite a good locality of the city. The only memory I have of my Mother is that she was an invalid, who suffered from TB and in those days there was no cure. She died when I was eight and I never really had the privilege of her love and care. It was not easy for my Father, two brothers or myself and the years ahead were hard. Knowing that her days were numbered, she began to wonder where she would spend eternity. I remember that once she sent for the local minister. I do not know how, but she eventually made contact with a spiritualist medium. I understand that there was the evidence of the supernatural and as a result my parents became involved in spiritism. Learning about some of these happenings and attending a couple of spiritist meetings only made me nervous and I never really became involved. There were times when one could sense a presence in our home and I never liked to be there on my own. Some of these things would have an influence upon me later in life as I would begin to learn from the Bible.

At the age of 20 my call up papers came through for National Service. The Army can lead some astray but I must confess that the discipline did me no harm and I began to live a more stable life. Eventually I joined as a regular soldier and was posted to Aden. The strong drink was cheap and much of my leisure time was at a bar. One day a friend played a joke on me. He had been invited by a Christian to come to his home for a chat. He asked me to come with him, no doubt for support, but he did not tell me that the couple were Christians. Not going empty handed, I took a few cans of beer with me and was shocked to find that they were Christians and members of SASRA. They did not partake of the beer but soon the conversation turned to the things of Christ and the Bible. I had never heard anyone talk like this before and could only wonder if they were all there. He gave me an invitation to come to a Bible study which was held at the Scripture Reader's home. Meeting other soldiers and airmen who knew the Lord helped me to begin to think. I began to attend the Bible study regularly and would often ask questions. Nearly always there was a good answer. For a while I tried to live a Christian life in my own strength and failed badly. The Scripture Reader knew about my problem and spoke with me at length. In the conversation he quoted *Revelation 3:16*. The Lord spoke forcibly to me from this verse. Being lukewarm was my problem and the Lord said ' You make me sick'. For a number of weeks I wrestled against it but one day I stopped where I was at work, gave in to the pleadings of the Holy Spirit, repented and accepted the Lord Jesus Christ as my Saviour. That was 1963. It was good to know His peace and joy that came into my life. I began to live a new life and the things that once held me down lost interest as I found the Lord to be so much better.

The Lord has wonderfully led over the years and I shall always be grateful for my army experience. The help and fellowship received through SASRA in those early days have been invaluable and being in the Forces taught me to stand and witness. Under normal circumstances I would probably have sat back and let more capable people do all the work. SASRA did not allow that. In most cases Scripture Readers knew how to get us to study the Word and to get us involved in the Lord's service. Quite often people would say to me 'Are you going to be a Scripture Reader?' I never felt that I was up to that challenge and therefore put it out of my head.

While serving at Tidworth I met a nurse, Barbara, who in 1969 became my wife. She also asked me if I was thinking of becoming a Scripture Reader. On the second week of our honeymoon we went to the Keswick Convention. The Bible Readings were in *2 Timothy* and the speaker brought out that Paul was telling Timothy he would have to carry on where he was about to leave off. He reminded us that someone had led us to faith in Christ and that we in our turn had to carry on with the Lord's work. The Lord could be calling you to the same kind of work. During this message I forcibly felt God's call to SASRA. The Scripture Reader who helped me in Aden was still fairly young and it would have appeared, still had a number of years to serve. He died quite young and literally we carry on where another had to leave off.

We both count it a privilege to serve the Lord in this way.

Mel Moodie joined the army in 1959, serving initially in the Cameronians (Scottish Rifles). Later he transferred to the Royal Signals where he served until April, 1970. His work as a Scripture Reader began in July, 1971.

28

Mrs Barbara Moodie

In my childhood I was blessed with a happy home and with loving caring parents. From the early age of three, I attended Sunday School and then Bible Class until I was seventeen. At my secondary school, we had Religious Education twice weekly and we were given a copy of the Bible, which I still have. We read the Scriptures and the RE Teacher would explain it. In the climate of our day, one can look back and be grateful for those days. At eighteen I left home to train as a nurse and saw much of the wrong side of our world. My background was to stand me in good stead and I still attended church with some of my colleagues, one of whom became a close friend. Through her testimony and in hearing a sermon one Sunday, I realised what was missing in my life. That I did not know Jesus Christ as my personal Saviour and that evening, asked Him into my life.

Completing my training and qualifying as a SRN, I then went on for further training as a Midwife. Prior to this I attended a Christian Convention in 1967 and was challenged through hearing a message on

Acts 9:6 and as a result offered myself for missionary service. At that time, I knew nothing of SASRA or of service life. While training in Salisbury, my friend and I met a Scripture Reader and his wife and often went to their home for fellowship. Through going there, I met a soldier who was a Christian and a SASRA member and who was to become my husband. On the second week of our honeymoon, we went to the Keswick Convention with the SASRA House Party. It was during this convention that we both felt called to the work of SASRA. My husband was still in the Army and I went with him to Germany which was a valuable experience. We had a Bible Study in our home which went very well and we were also called upon to run a Garrison Sunday School. During those days, we met up with other Scripture Readers and their wives and learned much from them about the work.

In 1971, my husband became a part time Scripture Reader and full time in 1972 at Catterick Garrison. Naturally, I have been involved with him in his work over the years. Whilst serving on the Salisbury Plain, we noticed that there were a number of Service women. In 1987, on hearing a message from *2 Samuel 15:15*, I applied to be a Lady Scripture Reader and for five years had the privilege of making visits to the girls. Our move to Scotland meant having to give it up as there are not the same amount of girls up here. As the wife of a Scripture Reader, I continue to support my husband in his work and have the privilege of leading a ladies' Bible Study Group and a ladies' Craft Group.

For a number of years now, I have worked as

a member of the team at the annual outreach to the men and women taking part at the Edinburgh Military Tattoo.

> *The Lord has blessed us with two children, Stephen and Esther, both of them are married. We have three grand children, Hannah, Nathanael and Josiah.*

29

ASR Jim Moore

I was born into a Christian home in 1939, the second of three children. My mother was a devout Christian woman, and my father, whilst not so devout, was supportive in her desire to raise the children as committed Christians.

The family were regular church goers and we attended faithfully the various in-church organisations. My mother took us along to the Christian Endeavour meetings and it was there on 24th September, 1952, that I put my trust in the Lord Jesus Christ as my personal Saviour.

I left Grammar School in June 1955 and after 18 months found myself serving in the Royal Navy. I joined as a Christian but soon found myself 'going cold at heart', mainly due to lack of fellowship. I served with the fleet around the world and in December 1960 married Gertie, who was a professing Christian. She had been saved in the Belfast City Mission in 1956.

My career continued to develop and in November, 1964, I passed the test for promotion to the commissioned rank of Sub Lt. I was ambitious to do well, but this had an adverse effect on my Christian testimony. I started to get my priorities wrong and spiritually was at a low ebb.

Following my commission in the Far East on board HMS Barrosa, I fell ill, and was invalided to hospital. Following medical tests it was established that I had contracted T.B. There followed a year of hospitalisation, ending in a medical discharge in December, 1965.

Two things were then apparent in my life. I was spiritually 'following afar off' and was young and ambitious enough to seek after the world's attractions. I tried several jobs and kept moving on because nothing seemed to satisfy me. In 1972 I joined the Royal Ulster Constabulary and served for six years during the troubles. I left in 1978 determined never to put a uniform on again.

During these years we had been blessed with two children, Stephen and Jennifer. Although spiritually in 'no man's land,' I was still a faithful attender at my local church but never feeling committed to it in the way I had been as a boy.

In early 1979 things began to change. I was offered a lucrative job in London and decided to accept it. Whilst the worldly ambition was there, deep down I felt uneasy about putting it in the place of my spiritual convictions. The Lord was working in my heart. In mid year, having decided not to change jobs, we did decide to move house. Moving to a new district necessitated moving church. We started to attend our present church, Christ Church Congregational on the outskirts of Belfast. God was moving and immediately, under the faithful ministry of the then Pastor, Rev Tom Shaw, I knew I had to get back to my first love. My wife Gertie and I did so and have been spiritually and materially blessed ever since. Out went the worldly ambition, in came a 'new vision' as to serving God.

Attending a meeting held in a church where there was a SASRA speaker, I knew God was calling me with my Naval/ RUC background to serve Him as an Army Scripture Reader. Ironically, in 1978, when handing in my police uniform, I had vowed never to don any uniform again. I learned a lesson then, that *'you never say never to God' Isaiah 55:8,9.*

In November 1982 I started to work as a part time Scripture Reader speaking to the men and women of the Royal Irish in St Patrick's Barracks, Ballymena where I continued to serve until my retirement.

In September 1986, I attended the Irish Baptist College full time and on completion, I became the Area Representative for SASRA in Northern Ireland.

I reflect over my life and praise God for His faithfulness to me, not least during the lean years, when I kept putting Him and His cause further and further down my personal agenda. I retired from SASRA in January 2005 and have been ordained in the Congregational Church in Ireland, in order to serve as an honorary Padre in the Air Training Corps.

Jim Moore served in the Royal Navy from 1957-1965. He began his work with SASRA as a part time Scripture Reader in November, 1982 and subsequently became the Area Representative for Northern Ireland in September, 1986, until his retirement in January, 2005.

30

Maj Gen Sir Laurence New CB CBE

I had just celebrated my 22nd birthday when, in late February 1954, I embarked on the Empire Windrush in Hong Kong, bound for the United Kingdom.

On the morning of Sunday 28 March an engine room 'explosion' awakened me at 0617. Wondering what had happened I put on slippers and a light dressing gown over my Shantung-silk pyjamas, and walked to the forward sun deck just below the bridge. Dense smoke was coming from the forward funnel. I vividly remember that the smoke suddenly turned to belching bright flame. My Royal Navy companion, with more experience of fire at sea, suggested that I might be wise to go back to my cabin and get dressed; but it was already too late as molten steel from the funnel was beginning to fall on the coach-top deck and set it alight. There was little we could do; there being no power and therefore no water. There were no tannoy messages because the system was dead; so there was no call to boat stations and there were no alarms being sounded. The ship was losing way and there was only a light breeze. I have a vivid recollection of seeing smoke coming from the voice pipes on the bridge and of hearing and actually seeing the Master call down to us from the open windows of the bridge to abandon ship. It was by now 0628. By 0640 the women and children and some male passengers were safely lowered into the sea and began to row away from the side of the hull. But the loss of power obliged us to lower the second tier of boats by hand. It was becoming clear that we would not achieve this before the lifeboat area was overtaken by fire so the decision was taken to push them overboard and allow them to fall some 60 feet into the sea where they could later be claimed. Most boats landed the right way up but some somersaulted and one or two landed on top of boats already pushed outboard.

By now the bridge and the sun deck were well alight, and the fire was advancing quite rapidly toward the bow. Clearly it was time to leave. Several of us made our way to the foredeck where we lashed some ropes, rope ladders and fire hoses to the starboard rail and threw over anything that would float. We then prepared to go over the side ourselves. This was the only unpleasant moment; it was a long way down! But any thought of staying seemed even less inviting! We clambered over the side at about 0645. Descending took a while, hand over hand on the rope ladder.

I was enormously relieved to discover that I wasn't scared out of my wits. I was also glad that there had been such an emphasis on swimming at my Isle of Man school, King Williams College – actually I had been awarded my First Colours for swimming only four years before this impending test! I swam towards a Carley float and hung on for a short time but it was already overcrowded. I recalled that a sinking ship sucks down those who are too close, so I began to swim away. The Windrush was now a sorry sight. It was already listing to starboard and burning from stem to stern; the compressed-air horn was continuing to moan. As I continued to swim I felt that it was time to take stock. It was definitely 'count your blessings' time. It was calm, it was daylight, the water was shark-free and not too cold; what more could one ask? I wished I had grabbed my life jacket before leaving the cabin but the thought that we might have to abandon ship had not crossed my mind at that stage. I would only be in serious trouble if I got cramp.

I don't know for how long I swam, but after a while I did what I should have done much sooner. I prayed! I asked the Lord, who I didn't know, to help me; and I accompanied this with an undertaking that if He would save me, I would make a very real effort to find and serve Him. I dare say that there were very few of us who did not murmur a silent prayer during those first hours; but I had made a promise.

After quite a while I looked up and saw in the distance a lifeboat that appeared to be empty. I began to swim towards it and eventually reached it. But hauling myself over the side proved impossible. The boat had obviously been one of those damaged when we were launching them; it was half full of water and appeared to have no oars or stores. I remember that several others eventually joined me. By then the boat lay lower in the water and we helped each other to scramble into it.

At about 1045, some four hours after we abandoned ship, four merchantmen came into sight. When they reached us they began to take the passengers on board. The 2,000 ton Dutch Cargo Vessel 'Mentor' (Captain Hazelhoss) manoeuvred along side us and we climbed gratefully up the companionway which had been rigged to the side of her hull. My pyjamas were still in place but not affording any privacy, so I welcomed the offer of a white boiler suit from the ship's Chief Engineer. Having given all my details to him and having downed some scalding coffee and some soup I readily accepted the offer of his bunk and slept very soundly.

Several days later we flew into Blackbushe airfield, and it was time to honour my promise to the Lord. I began to read the Bible and attend talks such as the '*ABC of Commitment*' by Lt General Sir Arthur Smith. I met military Christians notably at the Royal Military College of Science at Shrivenham. Thereafter, with my wife, I even ran a Bible Study House Group at the Staff College. But I still did not know Jesus as my personal saviour. Eventually, at about 30,000 feet in a RAF Andover on my way back from Africa, I was reading John Stott`s classic book 'Basic Christianity'. I was challenged by his description of Holman Hunt`s painting 'The Light of the World', a painting actually inspired by *Revelation 3:20, 'Behold I stand at the door and knock; if anyone hears My voice and opens the door, I will come in and sup with him and he with Me'*. John Stott posed the question 'Which side of your door is Jesus? Is he on the inside or the outside'. I saw in an instant that `although I had been praying, it had been through the keyhole. There and then

I asked the Lord to come in and take over my life completely. I saw it as a simple matter of command; I asked the Lord to become my Commander-in-Chief. The Lord graciously accepted this hesitant approach to His throne. Almost immediately, thanks to the Holy Spirit who 'leads us into all truth' (*John 16:13*), I understood the cross for the first time, and claimed Christ's substitutional atonement for myself (*2 Cor. 5:19*). An understanding of eternal life (*John 3:16*) and the fruit of the Spirit (*Gal. 5*) followed. For me the life-long sanctification walk had begun. Eighteen months later David Watson led my wife to the foot of the cross; we have been partners in the Gospel ever since. I was invited to join the SASRA Council that year and had the enormous blessing of a Scripture Reader, ASR Jim Kirk, in my command team both at Squadron and Regimental level. My testimony is that ever since then the Lord Jesus has been my keeper. His yoke is easy for His instructions are simple *'Follow me and I will make you to become fishers of men' (Matt. 4:19).*

Sir Laurence New, on graduation from RMA Sandhurst was commissioned into the Royal Tank Regiment in July 1954. He is married to Anna and they have four grown up children. He served as President of SASRA from 1985 until 1999 and is currently a Vice President. Sir Laurence served as HM Lt Governor of the Isle of Man from September, 1985 until September, 1990. He also served as Colonel Commandant of the Royal Tank Regiment from 1986 until 1993.

31

ASR Ernest Paddon

God is able to do exceedingly abundantly above all that we ask or think

It was at the 22nd milestone north of Rangoon in Burma when I read this verse in 'Daily Light'. We were surrounded by the Japanese and were considering the only option – surrender. None of us looked forward to a POW camp under the Japanese. Was God able? That night we heard gunfire. A Tank Corps had arrived from India over the Chindit Hills and battered down the roadblocks. We quickly escaped to freedom.

I joined the Army in 1940 and after a vehicle maintenance course, volunteered to serve abroad. Life in the Army was not easy. Although I became a Christian when I was 13 years old, my faith was strong. I found it difficult to openly confess Christ in the barrack room, so kept quiet. This made me feel uncomfortable but God is able and with His help, I was determined that when I was next posted I would stand up and be counted. The result was most encouraging and it was good to meet many Christians in this country and in India. It was there that I went to ASR & SACA meetings and also to the Agra convention.

During the next four years, besides being in Burma for some time, I was also posted to the Maldive Islands; N. W. Frontier; Kashmir and many other places. On V.E. Day I was in the Suez Canal on my way home and was demobbed a year later. I thought that was the end of my involvement with the Army.

I had considered going to India as a missionary but was turned down by a missionary society. Then I felt the Lord was leading me into teaching and after specialising in Religious Education I taught for the next thirty years in Comprehensive Schools and remain in contact with some whom I taught.

In Westminster Chapel where I am a member I was affected by a visit from Arthur Blessit when he asked, 'When did you last lead a soul to Christ?' I could not answer. As a result, 'Pilot Lights' (street witnessing) was started. I took an Evangelism Explosion course and became increasingly eager to evangelise. During this time Wellington Barracks was being rebuilt and Dr Kendall (our minister) commented that we had a mission field right on our doorstep. He was keen to go into the barracks himself but because he is an American and had not done military service, it was not possible. SASRA was contacted but had no one available and suggested that the Chapel might have a suitable person. After a meeting when Brian Henagulph and Brig Ian Dobbie spoke about SASRA, I felt the Lord was calling me to become a Scripture Reader. Margaret too, was feeling the same impulse. Contact was made with SASRA and after an interview with Col Sear and a written examination,

I spent a week with Mel Moodie on Salisbury Plain. Our visits to men in barrack rooms, guardrooms and hospital proved most helpful and I am grateful to Mel for his advice and guidance.

By this time Wellington Barracks was almost rebuilt and the 2nd Btn Coldstream Guards took up residence. I had an interview in April 1985 with the Senior Chaplain of London District and the Commanding Officer of the Battalion and they agreed to accept me as a Scripture Reader but limited me to the NAAFI. I was disappointed with this. God is able! After much prayer by the SASRA family the CO a month later gave me permission to go anywhere in Wellington Barracks.

What a great God we have and what a great privilege it is to speak to men about the things that really matter and to introduce them to the King of Kings; the Lord Jesus Christ. Over the years many have come to know the Lord as their Saviour. Some were heavy drinkers, some, like David, resisted for many years but ultimately became a Christian and was the means of bringing several members of his family to Christ.

Ernest Paddon served in the Army with the Royal Artillery and Royal Electrical & Mechanical Engineers between November, 1940 and November, 1946. He began his work as a Scripture Reader with SASRA in April, 1985 and retired from his appointment in June, 2000.

32

ASR Lee Philipson

When I was a young boy, my mother used to take my sister and I to a Baptist Church where we attended the Sunday school. During those years, I learned about the main characters and stories in the Bible: Creation, The Flood, The Tower of Babel, Sodom and Gomorrah, Abraham and Moses etc. I also learned about a place called Hell where all the bad people went and about Heaven where God lives. I heard enough about Hell to know that I did not want to go there and enough about Heaven to know that, that's where I would rather be. The way to get there, however escaped me. For I knew that all the wrong I did, which the Bible calls sin, kept me from gaining access to this place. Then, one day I discovered the way. I was reading John 3:16 and it was as if someone had turned on a light in my heart and mind. Jesus had paid the price for all my sin, all I had to do, was to earnestly ask God to forgive me all my wrongs and accept Jesus' sacrifice for myself and I would be saved! Therefore, this ten-year-old child, knelt by the side of his bed, asked God to forgive his sins and invited Jesus Christ into his heart to be his Saviour. My Mum was thrilled whereas my Father was indifferent. So began my walk as a Christian. The children at school noticed I would not swear and blaspheme so I was soon became known as "Brother Lee" after a TV character. I was aware of the need to confess Christ before others, so I began to witness to my friends at school. Obviously with the witness, came the persecution.

At 16 I joined the Royal Engineers and studied at the Army Apprentice College at Chepstow to be an Electrical and Mechanical Draughtsman. During my time there, the only spiritual influence was the occasional Church Parade. The Chaplain was a pleasant chap but we tended to see him only on rare occasions outside the church. For the first 12 months I cooled off my relationship with the Lord, not being helped by the little to no spiritual help or input from any other direction. After that 12 months cooling period I disposed of the NHS glasses and bought contact lenses. This was the beginning of a whole new social life but I no longer had the checks and balances in place to keep it at a sensible level. On being posted to Ripon, I began drinking heavily. Coupled with this was an attitude to sex and women that began to take over my life. My relationship with God was being more and more pushed into the background, though occasionally things would happen where He'd remind me that He was there and of my youthful commitment to Him. This helped to curb certain excesses but not all. Towards the end of my time in Ripon, I unwisely became unequally yoked to a non-believing lady from my hometown of Burnley. Though I gave up my womanizing ways when we married, sadly, for my wife, the grass was always greener on the other side.

On leaving the Army, we went to live with her parents. For work, I took a job in a textile factory. This proved to be hard, dirty work but at least there was a pay packet at the end of the week. Shortly after my wife asked me to leave, I moved back with my mother. When I said goodbye to my wife and young son, I was in total disbelief at what was going on. It was while I was at this low point of my life that I seriously began to look at what had happened and why? I realized I needed to sort out my relationship with my Father in Heaven – but how? On reflection, I could see that the trouble had started when I ceased to have fellowship with other Christians. I then made my mind up to seek out a true bible believing church, not one going through the motions but a real church where the Scriptures were taught. My mother had been looking for a new church and told me about some she had visited. One of them was a fellowship that met in a small hamlet, inside a barn. One Saturday, I told my Mum of my intentions to go on the Sunday and asked if she would go with me, to which she agreed. That Sunday morning, found me tentatively entering a barn, not sure what to expect. I could feel the difference straightaway! There was a sense of warmth in the place and I'm not talking about the heaters down the middle of the room. They started to sing choruses, as well as hymns. This was all new to me. It was the singing of a children's chorus, "Wide, wide as the ocean," that made the difference. When we reached the words "I though so unworthy, still am a child of His care,' it became clear to me that, though I had done my own thing and disobeyed His word, He still loved me and I was still His, for we are taught that nothing can separate us from the Father's love. On singing this chorus I felt an enormous rush from one end of my body to the other and tears streamed down my face. At that moment the prodigal son had returned and my heavenly Father had gathered me into His arms. I sought out two things straight away. Firstly, I decided I wanted to be baptized and renew my witness for Christ. Secondly, I wanted to know what the Bible had to say about divorce. After much reading, I discovered that, as my unbelieving wife was divorcing me, though it was not His perfect will, I was in His permissive will and that, as she wished to leave the marriage, I had to let her go. With this at least I had peace of mind as far as my relationship with the Lord was concerned.

As I began my witness for Christ, in the factory where I worked, one thing that was noticed immediately was that I had ceased to swear. I also had my Bible on the factory floor with me, which I read on my breaks. After the initial ridicule, the lads started to ask questions. At this time, I had a burden and desire in my heart that the Lord would somehow use me to encourage Christians in the Armed Forces in a way that I had never received. I did not know how He would do this but I was more and more convinced that this was what He wanted me to do.

In the nine years that followed, I grew in the Lord, attended a preaching course, taken from Spurgeon's "Lectures to my students" and was encouraged to preach the word in church, as well as outdoor speaking. During this period of spiritual growth, I re-married to a Christian lady called Debbie. I was blessed in the fact that I was able to baptize her in the village stream.

Whilst attending a church in Ripon, North Yorkshire, one of the members said he was going to a meeting in Harrogate, and would I like to come along? This I did. At the meeting I was pleasantly surprised to see a Brigadier of the Royal Engineers preaching the Gospel. It was a SASRA meeting and, as soon as I realized who and what SASRA was, I knew that this was the calling for which the Lord had been preparing me. After the meeting I made myself known to Brigadier Dobbie and to ASR Sinclair Quinn, who was also speaking and I was invited to apply for the position of Scripture Reader. Then followed three years of applications, praying, interviews and examinations; at the end of which I was welcomed into the ranks of Scripture Readers.

Lee Philipson joined the Army in July, 1990 and served in the Royal Engineers until November, 1991. He commenced his work as a Scripture Reader with SASRA in August, 2003. Lee is married to Debbie and he has four children, Ryan, Jonathan, David and Hannah.

33

ASR Sinclair Quinn

The outdoor life was the life for me. Football, squash, fishing, canoeing, mountaineering and parachuting were among the sports I tried in order to get a 'kick' out of life. I played squash nearly every day of the week. My skill at shooting was sufficient to win me medals. Every sport I tried was giving me satisfaction for a little while, but soon I was bored again and went on to something different. No matter what type of sport I tried, it never gave me any real or lasting satisfaction. In my heart I knew that there had to be something more fulfilling in life, though I hadn't the slightest idea what that something might be. Where was the lasting satisfaction to be found? How could I get the most out of life? Where could I find satisfaction? These were the questions to which I vainly sought an answer during the greater part of my earlier life. My parents could not answer these questions either even though they were God fearing people, with a great respect for the Gospel and they made me attend a place of worship.

All through my teens, I was really looking for

'something' and began drinking at an early age. What I didn't realise was that this 'something' was really 'SOMEONE' who had created and supports this universe. I didn't understand that this 'SOMEONE' whom we call God, not only permeates space but wants to take control of our lives. I married a girl from a Christian home. In her home I experienced an atmosphere I had never known before, it was real Christian love in a close knit family. This had a great effect on me and the upright manner in which my wife's uncle lived helped me to believe that the Christian message was true. I began to realise there was more to life than getting up in the morning, going to work, coming home, taking part in sport and going into a bar. In the end I didn't just go into a bar for a drink but with the intention of getting drunk.

One night the memory of past sins began to bother me and this went on for some time. I still would not face up to the fact that I was a sinner and my drinking habit became even stronger. One evening I went to see two friends who were Christians even though I was under the influence of drink. A strange thing happened. I am far from being an emotional man, yet the moment they opened the door to me I began to weep. They brought me in and began to speak to me of the greatest need in my life, which was to accept Jesus Christ as my personal Saviour from the power and punishment of sin and to commit my life to Him. Their words were wasted on me for I was wrongly counting on getting to heaven on my own merits. 'I've never done anyone any harm,' I told them. They invited me to a church service and I decided to go. I will always remember what they were singing as I entered the building. It was about Christ leaving the splendour of heaven to lay down His life for me at Calvary.

That was news to me. I had heard of Jesus Christ but, had not understood He had died for me, personally. I had been to Sunday School but I had never listened to my teacher. I didn't get converted to Christ at that stage in my life but, I realised the people in the church had something which I hadn't. This 'something' seemed very desirable to me but I did not know how I could obtain it. I knew that the world with its pleasures did not contain this. I kept on going to these services and asked my wife to go but she declined.

There were many of my friends and relatives praying for me and, probably in answer to their prayers, my sins troubled me so much that I couldn't sleep or eat. One night my wife did go to the Gospel service. Shortly afterwards, at half past five in the morning, she knelt at the side of the bed and repented of her sins and asked the Lord Jesus Christ to take control of her life. This had a great effect on me and I promised to help her all I could in her new life. Nevertheless, I still went on with my old sinful habits and I drank very heavily. Many a night I came home with no shirt on, battered and drunk.

To learn more about spiritual matters, I obtained some tapes which told how various people had come to know the Lord Jesus Christ as their personal Saviour. As I listened to these sincere and touching testimonies, I wept. On three occasions, I knelt beside my bed thinking of giving my life over to Christ but, pride and fear of what others would say and do kept me from going through with it.

Mentally, I was in a desperate state. I felt literally torn apart as one half of my being still craved for the pleasures of sin and the other half desired to get right with God. I did not know what was wrong with me. I have been speaking of my search for God but, it is more true to say that God was searching for me. Everywhere I turned, God was speaking to me through my different experiences in life. For instance, I read a book on Russia but, it contained more about Christ than communism. In despair, I thought about ending my life and rang the Samaritans to see if they could offer any help. They listened but could not drive the despair out of my mind.

At this time two elders of the church called to see me but, I resolved that whatever happened, I would not take part in any kind of religious conversation. They talked about everything under the sun and in the end it was I who began to speak about the Gospel. One of them talked to me and asked me a few questions. I agreed with all he was saying. Then he asked me, 'Would you like to give your life over to the control of Jesus Christ as your Lord and Saviour?' I knew then that a turning point in my life had been reached. I had to make a decision. I knelt down and prayed. Today, I do not remember what I said but, I knew I was converted to Jesus Christ. The old life had passed away and a new life had begun.

Sinclair Quinn served with the UDR in Northern Ireland prior to his conversion. He began his work with SASRA as a Scripture Reader in September, 1983. He is married to Valerie and they have two grown up sons.

34

ASR Mark Reynolds

In September 1971 I joined the Regular Army, aged 23, married to Jeanette and with two children, Paul & Andrew. Colin was to come later. Jeanette and I were not saved, although if anyone had asked me, I would have said that Jeanette was a Christian because she had the boys christened and she sometimes went to church. In 1978 I was posted to Bielefeld, Germany for the second time and during this posting our lives were to change dramatically.

A short time before I was saved, Jeanette was in the supermarket and saw someone in uniform. He was Derek Brooks, the Scripture Reader for 1(BR) Corps and Heather his wife was with him. They got chatting and invited Jeanette for coffee. She politely said that she would try to call, as she passed their home most days. One day, passing their house, she prayed, even though she was not then saved 'Lord, if I go to the Scripture Reader's, I want Mark to go with me because I just know I will be different and I want Mark to change too'.

A Christian S/Sgt from work lived in the next block of flats to us. In November 1979, I was ill at home with a very bad dose of the flu'. I asked Jeanette if she would pop across and see my S/Sgt for something to read. I liked science fiction or cowboy books but she came back with the 'Late Great Planet Earth' by Hal Lindsey. This was the book that God used to convict me of my sin and bring me to Christ. *Ephesians 2:8* was the verse that broke me that afternoon, 22nd November, 1979. I knelt down, weeping and asked the Lord to forgive my sin and come into my life. I got up and said, 'Lord, I do not know how to be a Christian, but I'm willing to try. You will have to help me.' When I told my S/Sgt what had happened, he said he would introduce me to a Scripture Reader. A few weeks later Derek Brooks was having a film night and my S/Sgt said, 'Why not take Jeanette along and we will baby-sit?` Jeanette came with me and to my surprise she already knew Derek. That night the film was about an RAF pilot and the text was *John 14:6*. It was this verse that brought Jeanette to a saving faith in the Lord Jesus Christ. When we arrived home that night, I said to Jeanette, 'Do you think it would be all right if we knelt beside our bed and prayed together?' This we did and what a joy it was.

Paul our eldest son came to Christ through the Sunday School that Derek and Heather ran. Andrew and Colin were saved through the children's work at SASRA's Easter Convention in Haus Stapelage.

At a SASRA Prayer Conference organised by Courtenay Harris, we felt the Lord clearly speaking to us from *Isaiah 62:10* and the vision we had then, which is just as strong now, was we believe, our call to SASRA. That we should be '*Signposts*' clear and easily read; '*Road builders*' working hard and patiently setting out the way of Salvation; '*Stone pickers*' removing stones of stumbling, using the word of God and of course '*Standard Bearers*' lifting up the Standard of Life '*I, if I be lifted up from the earth, will draw all men unto me*' John 12:32.

The Lord's timing in our lives is something we could not have planned. Jeanette and I feel very humbled by the Lord's goodness and grace to us. We are also most grateful for all the prayer and encouragement from so many people along the way.

Mark Reynolds served in the Territorial Army with the Royal Army Service Corps from 1965–1967 and then with the Kings Own Yorkshire Light Infantry from 1968–1971. He joined the Regular Army in September, 1971 with the Royal Corps of Transport, where he served until September, 1993, when he commenced his work with SASRA as a full time Scripture Reader in October, 1993.

35

ASR John Rowlands

I was converted in the October of 1954 as I listened to the preaching of Dr Billy Graham at a relay meeting from the Harringay Arena in the Royal Hall, Harrogate. At the time, I was a boy soldier at the Army Apprentices School (AAS), Harrogate, doing trade training as an apprenticed surveyor (Mapping). I had joined up in 1953 at age fifteen, straight from the Queen Elizabeth Grammar School in Carmarthen, South Wales. My father, Major Tom Rowlands, was serving with the Welsh Regiment as a Quartermaster, and I had it in mind to follow in his footsteps. My parents, though more nominal than practising Christians, had always encouraged me to attend a Sunday School and join the church choir whenever it was possible.

Upon my enlistment in 1953, I joined the Garrison Church choir and was confirmed by the then Bishop of Ripon. However, after initial training and trade selection, I was moved into the appropriate 'A Company' and found myself in a barrackroom amongst 29 other apprentices. In that room, I found myself opposite a lad called Michael Davies whose life style was in stark contrast to the rest of us. He never used bad language, never gambled, and went to church in Harrogate having already attended the Sunday morning Church Parade! We all considered him to be a religious fanatic when he openly read his Bible and witnessed to his faith in the Lord Jesus Christ. We were somewhat incensed by his inferences that we weren't really Christians, and many a time I found myself arguing against the challenge of the Gospel.

Curiosity, and the prompting of the Holy Spirit of God, caused me to accept an invitation by Michael to attend the Sunday afternoon young people's Bible Class at the Elim Hall (Brethren), in the Kings Road, Harrogate. Imagine my surprise at finding a number of other Army Apprentices in attendance. Though I found things strange, I kept on attending the Bible Class and evening Gospel meeting, mainly because of the hospitality offered for a 'nosh-up' in the homes of the folk in the fellowship. I was greatly impressed by their love and concern for us soldier boys and their manner of living, and soon found myself looking forward to spending Sundays at the Gospel Hall. Most Sundays, there were between 20 to 30 Army Apprentices in attendance, and 4 or 5 families invited us for tea each time.

One Monday night in October, 1954, Michael and I went to the Royal Hall in Harrogate to hear Dr Billy Graham, the place was packed and I sat and listened to a message used of God to change my life. I didn't 'get up and go forward', time was tight to get back to barracks. However, Captain

Cox (RAMC) a Christian Officer from the camp, took me aside following the Bible Study on Tuesday night and through the Word of God, explained the change I had experienced the night before. In the March of 1955, I requested adult baptism along with two other apprentices, and we were baptised by immersion in the Gospel Hall baptistry in obedience to God's Word.

It was in the Harrogate Gospel Hall that I met Audrey, and we kept in touch whilst I went on to serve in Cyprus, Iraq, and the Arabian Peninsula. The Lord was good throughout those dangerous years of service, and I can testify to His keeping power and that peace which passes all understanding. I returned from the Middle East in August 1959 following which Audrey and I were married in Harrogate in March 1960. I have never regretted our union and I thank God continually for Audrey's ministry to me and for the three lovely children He has given us.

After a spell as an instructor at the School of Military Survey, Newbury, I was posted to Singapore where Audrey joined me with newly born daughter Dawn. The years in Singapore were terrific as we came under the ministries of ASR Ted Frampton followed by ASR Bob Hodson and Harry Perrott of the Sandes Soldiers' and Airmen's Home. Then, convinced that we should leave the Army and prepare for Christian service, I went to the Moorlands Bible College near Dawlish, Devon for two years training, worked for Sun Life of Canada until 1969 and then took up the Superintendency of the Sandes Soldiers' Home on the Palace Barracks at Holywood in Northern Ireland, along with Audrey, Dawn and Stephen.

Our time at Holywood was very full and satisfying and after ten exhausting years we left the work, rejoining it in Catterick until that Home was sold in 1983. We returned to Harrogate where we spent a period running the Christian Alliance Hotel and Conference Centre and later joined SASRA in 1991. In London we have a dual role as the Area Representative and part-time Scripture Reader to the Household Troops in Central London. It is a privilege to represent the work to the Lord's people and also to minister as a Scripture Reader to the Guards Regiments.

John Rowlands served in the Royal Engineers from February, 1953 to August, 1964. He began his work with SASRA as Area Representative for the greater London Area and part time Scripture Reader to the Household Brigade in June, 1991. John is married to Audrey. They retired from SASRA in July, 2002.

36

Major Philip Shannon MBE

I was brought up in a Christian home in Northern Ireland where there was a love and reverence for the Bible and, from my earliest recollections, I remember attending Church and Sunday School. Along with my brother and sister, I was encouraged to learn verses of Scripture and to participate in all the youth activities associated with the Church. Each summer in the early 1960s, Child Evangelism Fellowship held a series of open-air meetings outside our home attended by many local children. We enjoyed the Bible stories and once again were encouraged to commit to memory key verses of Scripture. One such verse was *John 3:16 'For God so loved the world, that He gave His only begotten Son, that whosoever believeth on Him should not perish but have everlasting life.'* The evangelist explained that it was because of our sin that Jesus came to this earth to die for us. All we had to do was accept Him into our lives and we would experience forgiveness and everlasting life. At the age of seven I realised that although I had not been particularly sinful, I still needed to make a decision regarding God's offer of salvation. Towards the end of a series of meetings, I took that vital step and invited Christ into my life.

At the age of fifteen, I decided to join the Army as a Junior Musician with the Royal Artillery in Woolwich. ASR's Frank and Vera Crofts had established contact with the regiment a few years earlier and a weekly Bible study was held not far from the barracks. They showed films on camp and soon other Junior Musicians began to attend. Some of them became Christians and we received encouragement and support from SASRA. When the Crofts were posted, they were replaced for a short time by ASR Gerald McClelland, after which a local man named Gerald Fiddler who had become a Christian while serving in Singapore in the 1950s heard of this small group and kindly assumed responsibility for the leadership until ASRs Ted and Lily Frampton came to the London area.

For us as a group of seventeen-year-old lads, we were fed from the Word of God each week and these became times of building up in the faith. I was soon posted to The Royal Military School of Music, Kneller Hall in Twickenham for a year's course where another Bible study group met regularly. The Framptons faithfully fought their way through the heavy London traffic just to continue to nurture us in God's word.

On returning to Woolwich and the Royal Artillery Band in 1975, I had the opportunity of travelling throughout the length and breadth of England giving concerts with both the band and orchestra. At every opportunity, I would try to accompany the

Framptons when they spoke at meetings and they always encouraged me to play my violin and lead for them. Once again I thank God for their wise counsel and Godly example.

Weekly Bible studics and the monthly SASRA prayer meeting in the Frampton's home near the barracks were times of real spiritual blessing. Quite often as many as twenty five people would crowd into their small front room and it was the place where young Christians gained the confidence to pray audibly for the first time. On their retirement, Ted and Lily were replaced by ASRs Joe and Jackie Smalley who continued the work in the area.

I met Elizabeth my wife at an Irish Christian Fellowship weekend in Herne Bay Conference Centre in 1978 and we were married in 1981. Like me, she had committed her life to God as a child and in her teens worked for a time with a Christian organisation in Ireland called Postal Sunday School. From Woolwich we were posted to the Royal Military School of Music, Kneller Hall; where I attended the three year Student Bandmaster course. We were greatly encouraged by another Christian Student Bandmaster and his wife who, with ASR John Dunbar, hosted a weekly Bible study.

In 1985, I was appointed Bandmaster of The 1st Battalion The Royal Regiment of Wales (24th/41st Foot), and we were posted to Germany, Wiltshire, Hong Kong and Shropshire. While in Germany our son Peter was born with a heart problem and was immediately flown home for emergency treatment at Guy's Hospital. As his life hung precariously in the balance both Elizabeth and I experienced the peace that only God can give in such a situation. Many friends, along with our families prayed for his recovery and after an anxious time we learned that the doctors could find nothing wrong with him. ASR Derek Brooks, along with his wife Heather were a particular help during that time and along with the SASRA fellowship in Herford, constantly supported us through the difficult time. We believe God miraculously honoured those prayers. Today, we have three children, all of whom have committed their lives to following the Lord Jesus Christ.

In 1994, I was commissioned and assumed the position of Director of Music of the band of The Prince of Wales's Division (Clive), based in Shropshire. It was also a particular honour to become a SASRA Council member at that time. Four years later, I was appointed to the band of the Welsh Guards in London. During this time, I travelled extensively and often found myself providing music for Her Majesty The Queen and other members of the Royal Household.

It has been a privilege to serve God in the Armed Forces and over the years my family has received much support from local churches, Scripture Readers and Chaplains. Having worked particularly closely with many Scripture Readers, I have observed how they have sought to present the Gospel to those who do not know of God's saving power and, to encourage and build up Christians in their faith.

There is a God-shaped blank in each of our lives which only God can fill. John 3:16 is as relevant today as it was all those years ago when I first learned it as a child clearly and simply showing how the God of love sent His only Son into a world that rejected Him. Jesus did not promise that the Christian life was going to be easy but, it is the most rewarding and satisfying life one could desire. What a privilege to know the saving and keeping power of this wonderful God who did not just **reach** down into this world but **came** down in the form of His Son, the Lord Jesus Christ.

Philip Shannon joined the Army in September, 1971 and was commissioned as a Director of Music in June, 1994. He also became a member of the SASRA Council in October, 1994.

37

ASR Ivor Sherwood

I was brought up in a Christian home in a little village near Andover in Hampshire. I was taken to Church and Sunday School each Sunday. Within the fellowship we had a Caravan Mission to Village Children. The Missioner was Joe Bush. It was during one of his missions in the village Chapel that I gave my life to the Lord Jesus Christ at the age of nine. Things were very easy for me then, living in a Christian family and having many Christian friends around.

In 1954 I was called up for my National Service and joined the Royal Hampshire Regiment. I spent most of my two years in Malaya leaving the Army in 1956 and returned to the Post Office. I found my time in the National Service difficult, in so far that there were no other Christians (that I was aware of) in my company, but I was able to attend Venning Road Chapel in Kuala Lumpa. On leaving the Forces I married May in 1957. I had a call to become a Scripture Reader and so re-enlisted in the Forces, in order to complete nine years service which at that time was necessary. I ended up doing 22 years.

Over those years we were posted to many places and enjoyed them all. My life as a Christian was not all it could have been but, I thank the Lord that He never left me nor forsook me and has indeed kept us both. We have three grown up children. Ann who is a schoolteacher in London; Keith, married to Sue with daughter Lauren, (Keith works with computers); Rebecca married to Michael, with Bethany, Nathan and Abigail, (Michael works in a bank).

When I finally left the Services I had two different jobs and after two years applied to SASRA for an Area Representative's post that was vacant. On being accepted I was four and a half years the Representative for the North of England. As I look back I thank God for this time of service which helped me in my relationships as a Scripture Reader.

I became a Scripture Reader in February, 1985 and was posted to Celle in Germany. Since then I have worked at five different locations and now serve in Rheindahlen. We have much for which to praise the Lord over these years. He has been faithful and true to us in all things. We enjoy serving Him and pray that we might continue to do so faithfully.

Ivor Sherwood joined the Army in 1954 as a National Serviceman in the Royal Hampshire Regiment. After a brief period in civilian life, he re-enlisted into the Royal Engineers where he served until 1979. His work with SASRA commenced as the Area Representative for the North of England in March, 1981. He later transferred to the role of full time Scripture Reader and retired from SASRA in July, 2001.

38

ASR Paul Somerville

Many years ago, a lady was a passenger on a coach that was travelling from Northern Ireland to the Republic, when it was stopped at a British Army checkpoint just inside the border. As she glanced through the window, she noticed a soldier standing by the side of the road, so young and so alone. She began to pray for him, for his safety and for his security and that somehow, somewhere, he would come into contact with the Gospel and be wonderfully and truthfully saved. It was then that she began to think of her own son, he too being a soldier but, stationed in a foreign land and still unsaved! Who was praying for him she thought, would he ever come into contact with the Gospel, would anyone speak to him about his need of salvation? Just then the coach pulled away to continue its journey south and the lady waved to the young soldier leaving her thoughts with the Lord.

I wonder have you ever thought what God can do with a life that is **prayed** into His hands? I was that soldier stationed in the foreign country and the lady on the coach was my mother who patiently cried unto the Lord that her soldier son would be saved and used of God.

When I enlisted into the Army in the mid 1980s, I found myself leaving behind a Godly home and embracing an environment far from the Christian upbringing that I had experienced. The only 'Christian' contact I had during my service days was when I was home on leave. Even then my church attendance was out of mere duty to my Mother rather than a heart felt desire to worship God. It was whilst home on leave after a tour in the Falkland Islands, that I found myself in the Sandes Soldiers' Centre in Palace Barracks. There I met a Scripture Reader named Sinclair Quinn, who chatted to me about the Lord Jesus Christ. Before we parted company, he challenged me about my 'standing before a Holy God.'

I returned to Germany several days after this encounter with the conversation still 'buzzing around' in my head. Upon arrival in Germany, I was briefed on the increased security state and soon found myself on a continuous cycle of guard duties. It was on one of these duties, that I began to seriously assess my own life. Deep down I was really troubled, for I knew that as a non-Christian, I did not have a future. A Scripture text that I learnt in my youth flashed across my mind, *Jesus said .. I am the way, the truth and the life, no man cometh unto the Father but by Me.' John 14:6.*

I had heard the Gospel story many times before but, that evening the Holy Spirit convicted me of my sin and I repented. I not only received a great Saviour by faith that night but, also a great peace, a great joy and, a great prospect.

As a young Christian Serviceman, I was indebted to SASRA for their fellowship and support and especially ASR Bob and Barbara Hodson for their counselling and guidance during those early years. When I left the Army in the Autumn of 1989, I returned to Northern Ireland. It was there that I was introduced to Jim and Gertie Moore, the SASRA Area Representatives for Northern Ireland, who lovingly continued to encourage me in my Christian walk. Jim challenged me about serving the Lord as a part time SASRA Reader and after much prayer, I made application and, praise God, I was accepted. I spent the first six years visiting RAF Aldergrove and then moved to Palace Barracks, in Holywood.

I had travelled a full circle from that place where the Gospel had been once preached to me several years before and, now I had returned to proclaim the same life saving message.

I have counted it a privilege to be called by God to work within SASRA, to enter both RAF stations and Army camps so that those 'in Christ Jesus' would be encouraged and, that those 'without Christ' would be enlightened but supremely that 'He might have the pre-eminence.'

Many years ago a lady was sitting in her home, when her son who was stationed in a foreign country telephoned. Her eyes filled with tears when she heard the words that her heart had so longed to hear, 'Mum, I have trusted the Lord tonight'...

Remember ...

'The effectual fervent prayer of a righteous 'man' availeth much.' James 5:16.

Paul Somerville, who is married to Gillian, served in the Royal Signals from November, 1985 to September, 1989. He began his work as a part time Scripture Reader with SASRA in February, 1992. In January, 2005, Paul became Area Representative for Northern Ireland, while continuing his Scripture Reader Ministry. They have one son, Aaron.

39

ASR Alastair Stewart

*O satisfy us early with thy mercy; that we may rejoice
and be glad all our days*

Psalm 90:14

The words of Scripture, *'O satisfy us early with Thy
mercy;'* used to hang on my bedroom wall in Edinburgh
and are one of my earliest memories. My Mother
ensured that I faithfully attended Sunday School but,
despite winning prizes for Bible knowledge, I used to
give my Sunday School teacher a hard time by being
inattentive and asking awkward questions. I used to
steal money out of my Mother's purse and deny all
knowledge of it when challenged. When I was twelve,
I went to listen to a minister preach in a local church,
which was different to the one I normally attended. I
was greatly surprised to discover that he was a blind
man and inwardly, I thought he ought to be blaming
God, not praising God because he was blind. That
evening he preached from *Revelation 3:20* and as he
made the Gospel message clear, I became conscious
of my sins, particularly stealing and lying. At the
close of the service, being under conviction of sin,

I sought counsel from the blind minister. I told him that I would like to become a Christian boy and that I would like to have the Lord Jesus Christ living in my heart. It gave him great joy to point me to the Saviour.

In the course of time, I was called up for National Service at the age of nineteen, in January 1958. I remember being a very quiet Christian and occasionally plucking up enough courage to speak up for the Lord Jesus Christ. I was greatly helped by the fellowship and ministry at the Gospel Hall whilst serving in Floriana, Malta in 1959/60. My National Service was extended to nine years service at the Lord's leading. My first contact with SASRA was in 1961 and I became a serving member in 1962. I enjoyed good fellowship with Scripture Readers Brown and Frampton in Aden in 1964/65. These were tremendous years for fellowship and corporate witness at RAF Steamer Point and we knew much of the Lord's blessing. I finished my RAF service in 1967 and, following two years as a student at the BTI Glasgow and a further year working in a Glasgow church, I responded to the call of God and applied to SASRA for a full time Scripture Reader post.

I was accepted and the Lord encouraged me as I started six months training in 1970 with the word's of *Psalm 118:6. 'The Lord is on my side, I will not fear, what can man do to me?'*

Pat and I were married in January 1971, and we began our joint service with SASRA the following month. (We had met while we were students at the Bible Training Institute.)

Looking back over our ministry with SASRA

in England, Scotland and Germany, I can truly praise God for His enabling when my own natural temperament was to be fearful. He has wonderfully come to my aid with His gracious help and strength. Over the years two verses from the book of *Proverbs* have been relevant in my situation. *'The fear of man brings a snare' (29:25) and 'In the fear of the Lord there is strong confidence' (14:26)*. Praise God that a healthy fear of God puts the fear of man into proper perspective.

Finally, I return to the verse which began this testimony and in particular, the second part of the verse, *'That we may rejoice and be glad all our days'*. These were the words that were not included on the wall picture in my bedroom as a child. How I praise God for His goodness in drawing me to Himself early in life, for preparing me during my time in the RAF for future service and for providing a wife, who also had a sense of call into the work of SASRA. We praise Him for all that is past and trust Him for all that's to come.

Alastair Stewart served in the Royal Air Force from January, 1958 to February, 1967. He began his work as a full-time Scripture Reader with SASRA in February, 1971 following his six months training period. Alastair and Pat retired from SASRA in October, 2003. They are now happily settled in Bridgend, Mid-Glamorgan.

40

Mrs Pat Stewart

I was brought up in Cardiff and at the age of seven, was invited by school friends to a Baptist Church. It was through the example and teaching of a godly Sunday School teacher and Girls Life Brigade leaders, that I first came to hear and understand the Gospel. At the age of fourteen, I responded to the invitation to trust Jesus Christ as my Saviour and later that same year, I was baptised. Although I was very sincere at that time, there was no real conviction of sin and little growth spiritually in the ten years following my baptism. In God's mercy and goodness He kept His hand upon me and though I was all too ready to wander away from Him during those years, every now and again, I was confronted with the claims of Jesus Christ upon my life. In 1965, still intent on going my own way, I headed out to Germany to teach primary age Army children at Herford under the auspices of BFES. (British Forces Educational Service). I still attended church on a Sunday morning but my heart was far from God. I was happy to be fully involved in the social life that was part of the 'officer status' afforded to teachers. Out of a staff of thirty there was one Christian teacher who, on finding out my background, invited me to SASRA bible studies and the Sunday Fellowship meetings. Initially, I made all sorts of excuses but, after some months, I began to see the emptiness of the pleasures I was supposedly enjoying. I also realised that my life was on a downhill slide. Late one night I cried out to God for help. The following day, I went to my Christian friend, Sylvia and told her that I would go with her the following Sunday to the SASRA Fellowship at Bielefeld. The Scripture Reader at that time was Frank Crofts and his wife Vera. For me, that Sunday was like coming home to where I really belonged. I was so challenged and humbled to hear young soldiers speak of their lives changed by Jesus Christ. This experience for me was the beginning of God revealing afresh His grace and love to me and of my realisation of my own sinfulness. At one meeting in particular it was summed up in the words of this hymn.

'I stand all amazed at the love Jesus offers us
Confused at the grace that so fully He proffers me
I tremble to know that for me He was crucified
That for me, a sinner, He suffered, He bled and died.
Oh it is wonderful that He should care for me enough
*   to die for me*
Oh it is wonderful, wonderful to me.'

Frank and Vera Crofts were followed by Jim and May Kirk and, I am so thankful for their Biblical teaching and example during my 2½ years in the SASRA Fellowship. The Lord promises to guide our steps and from Germany, I was led to the 'Bible

Training Institute' in Glasgow from 1968 – 1970. It was there that I met Alastair, who was later to become my husband. Our mutual interest in the work of SASRA was all part of the plans and purpose of God. His ways are higher than our ways. He brought us together and called us into the work of SASRA in 1971. It is a joy to record that He not only called us but, He has kept us and we would seek to give Him all the glory.

Pat and Alastair have been blessed with two grown up sons, John, who is married to Kristine and Andrew, who is married to Nicola.

41

ASR William Wade

"You're all sinners!" The pastor of the little Elim Pentecostal Church was passionate as he preached. I had no problem with being called a sinner. By the time I was hearing these words from a converted bar manager, now a church planting preacher, I was in a world of trouble. I had not long been charged with assault and criminal damage, to go along with other similar criminal offences, mainly alcohol related. I had tried, but without success, to finally put glue sniffing behind me. The drinking was out of control too, and it was all catching up with me. I was involved with the National Front and on the fringes of Paramilitary activity. I had no doubt that I was a sinner. What the preacher said next gave me something that would ultimately change my life forever. "But I want you to know that God loves you."

There were around six or seven of us there that night, in the Jubilee Hall, in the centre of Greenisland housing estate. The church itself only had around ten or twelve as a congregation, so we almost doubled the attendance. We all sat along the back row, and laughed our way through the choruses and notices, but when the preacher stood up to preach, we all fell silent. It was a bizarre situation. He was actually making sense out of life. It was when he began telling us that God loved us and that Jesus Christ His Son died for us in order that we might have eternal life that I began to think of where I would be in five or ten years' time. It didn't look good. I was being offered a way out of the life I had come to live, but it wasn't an easy way, it was the way of surrendering my life completely into the hands of God and becoming, as the preacher said, a "born-again Christian".

It was a folly of events that got us all to that hall in the first place. My friends and I were having a little bit of a party in my sister's house on the estate one Saturday night. It was around 9 or 10pm when their door was knocked. Standing there were two girls we knew from the estate. They asked if they could come in. We weren't going to say no! We didn't expect what happened next, though. They began to talk to us about God, about Jesus Christ and about being "saved". They had been saved and their lives were evidently different than they used to be. Even though we were all sitting around drinking and making fun of these two girls, they weren't put off and kept telling us of the love of God. They eventually left and challenged us all to come to the evening service at their little church. In order to get rid of them, we said yes. We didn't plan bumping into them the next night, just before the evening service, but that's exactly what happened. Using every kind of excuse, we said no but they wouldn't take no for an answer. We decided to go, to disrupt the service, but had no idea that we were the ones who would be disrupted!

The pastor preached a straight Gospel message to us all, but none of us responded. We tried to act hard and unaffected after the meeting, but I had been convicted. The same thing happened the week after. Saturday night – drunk, Sunday night – at the meeting. The following Thursday, a few of us had a chat with the two girls and the subject of Heaven and Hell arose. Again, I realised from what these girls had told us and what the pastor had preached, I was heading for Hell because I had never asked Jesus Christ to be my Lord and Saviour. These two girls spoke about Heaven with such a certainty that I wanted to go there, but I knew I needed to get "right with God" as they put it. I decided that I would respond to the appeal on the following Sunday night. We all went again, and the pastor faithfully preached a simple Gospel message that we could understand. After the message, he asked us all to bow our heads and close our eyes. He asked if there was anyone who would like to give their lives to Christ, and if so, could they raise their hands. My heart was beating like mad. What would my mates think? Could I keep up the Christian faith? What about my family? All of these questions seemed to disappear as I thought about a life in God. As I was getting ready to raise my hand, one of my friends raised his! I couldn't believe it! I was next, then another two of my friends indicated the same. Four of us in one night. The pastor took each of us into a little room off the main hall and explained a little bit more to us of what salvation actually meant. He then led us, line by line, in a prayer of repentance, as we didn't know how to pray ourselves. The only way I can describe how I felt was that for the first time in my life I felt clean. It was like I had been washed from the inside. I knew God had done a work in my life.

A lot has happened in my life since then. I have spent seven years as a soldier in the Royal Irish Rangers Regiment. I have also completed a two-year residential Bible Study course, which is where I first met Tulsi. Tulsi and I have been married for seven years and we have been working for SASRA for three years. As I go around the Barrack rooms here in Rheindahlen Germany, I am constantly reminded of the state I was in when God began to speak to me about salvation. This is the message I bring to soldiers, no matter what background or religious affiliation, Jesus Christ died for every one of them, for He died for sinners. I am testimony to that.

William Wade served in the Royal Irish Rangers from 1989 until 1992 following which he attended Bible College from 1994–1996. In 1998 he rejoined the Army serving in the Royal Irish Regiment until 2001. William began his work as a Scripture Reader with SASRA in November, 2001. He is married to Tulsie and they have one daughter, Micah.

42

ASR Nick Wilson

I was born in Shortlands near Bromley, where I spent the first four years of my life. When my sister Penny was expected, we moved to an enormous house in Beckenham. My Father, Dennis Wilson, was in the BBC Show Band and doing much freelance piano playing, including 'The Goons,' while my mother Betty worked in overseas research for the BBC at Bush House. I can remember parties going on downstairs for show business personalities and musicians. On one occasion Robert Farnon came downstairs and announced he had just seen a small boy running around upstairs with no clothes on – me aged five years!

We lived opposite an Anglican Church. My Mother showed me a 'Him' Book and 'Priy' Book I had written when five years old, including the Lord's Prayer. 'Our Father, which art in Heven, Harlard be Thy name!' My Father left home for good on my sixth birthday. Mother went to see the Vicar for his advice, which was never to divorce. She did her best to bring up my sister and I and so it was, that after a period of two years we moved to Kingsdown near Deal, by which time I was eight years old. My sister went to Dover Grammar and I went to Dover College. Kent County Council advised that I should be a boarder and paid the difference in school fees. Subsequently in 1965 we moved to Ringwould about a mile away.

I was not bright and have been struggling with literacy and reading music for fifty-four years. During this time I went through many religious phases, not least singing treble, followed by alto and tenor in the Chapel Choir over a period of five years. We sang Evensong in quite a few Cathedrals including Winchester, Chichester and Ely. I listened to all the sermons preached at Matins on Sunday mornings intently. Father Joe from the East End of London came for one week of mission and I was deeply moved. It was my ambition to play the flute with my Father who had moved into composing and arranging for television. He had written the music for 'Till Death Us Do Part, Faulty Towers, Steptoe and Son' and numerous others.

Our entire family has been in the military. My Father served in the Royal Army Pay Corps in India during World War 2, while back home, my Mother flew Spitfires and Hurricanes and was in charge of delivering military vehicles across the United Kingdom. In more recent times my sister served in the Wrens and for a time, was a member of the Royal Marines' Freefall Parachute Team. It was my Mother who suggested that I should join an Army Band, which I did in September 1969 when I signed on in the Royal Artillery Band in Woolwich.

I enjoyed my time in the Royal Artillery Bands

in Woolwich, Dortmund and Larkhill. After eight years, I felt an emptiness in my life and believed I had achieved nothing. My only bad experience was playing at a State Banquet in Luxemburg. I had a sixteen bar solo at the end of a 'Tchaikovisky' piece when I had a panick attack and it sounded like 'Schoenberg'. The Queen was not amused and the Director of Music did not speak to me for several days. Our band was also booked to do fourteen concerts in a week at the Embankment Gardens in London. I was so terrified at the prospect; I bought myself out of the Army. Years later, a friend of mine in the band told me that I should not have worried since at the first concert there was only one person in the audience. After playing two numbers, the Director of Music asked if he would like to hear any special piece of music. 'I am the Park Keeper just waiting to lock up!' After a few weeks on the dole, I took a job as a Home Care Advisor (Brush Salesman). Within five months of leaving, I decided to rejoin the Army this time in the Band of the Scots Guards. This was a new experience with all the additional kit cleaning! I was very grateful to the Director of Music, Duncan Beat, for accepting me and so glad I completed my twenty-two years.

Now I was a little more contented with my life but had no peace with God or myself. In 1980, the Jehovah Witnesses came to my door in Forest Hill. Because of my total lack of Bible knowledge, I studied their 'Truth' book for one year. During the summer of 1981, a very close friend of my Father's rang up to advise me to give up studying with them, which I agreed to do. In August 1981, the Scots Guards

Band went to take part in the Edinburgh Military Tattoo. On the first day of rehearsals at Redford Barracks, I saw a notice that pointed to SASRA – 'SAS Royal Artillery' – 'I must investigate,' I thought and entered the SASRA Room, where I immediately felt a calm and peace I had never experienced before.

ASR Alistair Stewart greeted me with no pressure and explained the use of the room. I told my friend Ray in the band, who had also been seeking the Lord for sometime, about the room. Alistair saw Ray and I waiting at a bus stop, to go into Edinburgh and invited both of us to tea on Sunday, then on to Charlotte Baptist Chapel for the Evening Service. The Gospel Service made an impression upon us and we both accepted an invitation from Murray Leitch to go to an evangelistic meeting conducted by Evangelist Dick Saunders in a large tent on the Meadows. I was not interested in the large choir or excellent pianist but wanted the message to begin. Something wonderful was going to happen that night. It did! Jesus spoke to my soul and forgave all my sins, past, present and future. He took me off the broad road that I saw I was on, leading to Hell and onto the narrow road that leads to Heaven. It is a wonderful free gift that cannot be earned, just accepted with everlasting praise and thanks. Ray and I both walked to the front and were then taken to meet a Counsellor, who kept in touch with us for six months to see that we were growing in the Lord. It was a fairly chilly night but that was not the reason I was shaking violently. Eight years of intense persecution followed. The Lord brought me through it all and I learned many lessons that I can now share with those going through trials. My Mother thought it was just another phase but twenty-one years later she saw that my faith was still growing. She wanted to earn her own way to heaven. I was given five minutes to talk at her funeral. 'I know what you Evangelicals are like,' quipped our good friend John Winn, who took the service at Ringwould Parish Church. Only twice did I manage to share my faith with my Dad. The first time he got up and walked away while my second opportunity came when he was in hospital after another stroke.

A source of real encouragement to me at that time was the weekly services held in the Guards' Chapel, Wellington Barracks in London. The Chaplain and Commanding Officer of the Coldstream Guards convened these events. Among those who were invited to preach was Evangelist, Dr Billy Graham. I took the opportunity to ask him if he still became nervous when preaching, to which he replied that he went in shaking every time, which gave me hope for the future.

The Scots Guards Band took on the role of nurses in Saudi Arabia in the first Gulf War. Many of the band laughed at me in training, as I could not manage one press up. 'Come on 'Godfrey,' keep up,' the Director of Music kept saying! He often used to ask at meal times how God was today? When we arrived, many of the band wanted to share a room with me. Chris started asking me questions about my faith and eighteen months later came to know the Lord. Many asked me why I was so content, to which I replied, 'because I know the Lord Jesus Christ as my Saviour.'

I met ASR Ernest Paddon and ASR John Rowlands who visited Wellington Barracks and attended most of the Bible Studies. They both said I should start thinking and praying about becoming a Scripture Reader when I left the Army, since they were both heading towards retirement! After a period of seven years, in March 2000, I applied and was accepted as a Part-time Scripture Reader with responsibility for visiting Wellington Barracks. During these past four years, I have enjoyed many valuable conversations with men in the barracks and sensed in an increasing way, God's seal on my call. As a result I was accepted as a full time Scripture Reader Evangelist and started my training in January 2005. It is true to say that I have no confidence in myself but every confidence in the Lord for the future.

It was at Westminster Baptist Church that I first met my wife Dolly, who has been a great blessing in my life. The Lord has blessed us with two children, Suzanne and Robert. My prayer is that the Lord would be pleased to use us as a family to bring Him much glory and honour through our service for Him in the ranks of SASRA.

Nick Wilson served in the Royal Artillery Band from September, 1969 until March, 1977. He rejoined the Army and served in the Scots Guard's Military Band from October, 1977 until November, 1992. His SASRA service began as a part time ASR at Wellington Barracks London in March, 2000. He became a full time Reader on 1ˢᵗ January, 2005. Nick is married to Dolly and they have two children, Suzanne and Robert.

43

Squadron Leader Colin R Woodland

My earliest recollections include attending Sunday school, firstly at a church in Rochester where the priest wore a funny little hat and a flowing black gown. When our family moved to Chatham, I attended Sunday school at the church in the village of Luton where the rector appeared only for services and always seemed to be dressed in a white blouse over his black flowing gown.

Throughout my Sunday school years, the one thing that came across loud and clear was that to attain a place in heaven I had to be good enough to be acceptable to God. I did all that I could think of to be good enough: I joined the choir; I became a server in the sanctuary at communion; I rang the church bells, I attended every service that I could. I would be at the early morning communion; the morning service; the Bible class and the evening service every week. By the time I was 14, I realised that all the wrong things I had done could never be cancelled out by the few good things I had done. I stopped going to church and concentrated on my lucrative paper round. When I joined the Royal Air Force, in 1960, I decided to give church another go. I became involved in Gregorian chanting and great rituals. Again, however, I recognised that the few good things I did at church could never compensate for the way I lived the other 6 days of the week. By the time I graduated from training at RAF Halton, I realised that hell was what I deserved and I could do nothing about it. So, on posting to RAF Ballykelly in Northern Ireland, I became a Sunday school teacher in the hope that I could convince young children to live a better life than I had done and avoid going where I was destined.

Then, one night, after hearing for the umpteenth time the story of the Prodigal Son, an elderly lady asked me a simple question, "Are you a Christian?" I answered, "Yes" because I thought everyone born into my society was a Christian, whether good or bad. However, her second question made it obvious she did not agree, "How long have you been a Christian?" I fobbed her off with a feeble "Since I was 7 ½."

From that moment on, I knew there had to be something more to being a Christian that being born into a nominally Christian society. I returned to my living quarters and knelt by my bed. "God," I said, "please make me a Christian." – Nothing seemed to happen and I got into bed.

Nevertheless, God was at work. The Bible says, "Everyone who calls on the name of the Lord will be saved." (Romans 10:13). Over the next few weeks, God revealed to me **His** plan of salvation and how it differed from mine. When Jesus was nailed to the cross, He became sin for us, He bore the sin of the whole world in His own body. My sin was included! Jesus paid the price of my sin for me. It is not a matter of how good I have been but how much I trust Him. It became clear to me that I could never, ever, be good enough to enter heaven, my rightful end was hell. But, Jesus paid that price for me. If I repented (was truly sorry for the wrong I had done; hated what I had done and wished I could take it back and make it undone); if I threw myself on His mercy; if I believed that His sacrifice was for me and if I believed that He rose again from the dead, He would forgive me. He would separate me from my sin "As far as the east is from the west" (Psalm 103:12). He would choose to remember my sins no more (Jeremiah 31:34). The Bible says that through Him I can know the truth and that truth would make me free (John 8:31-32).

Suddenly, the light dawned. It is not a matter of what I have done for God but what God has done for me. I am not worthy of a place in heaven **but** God has made me worthy of a place in heaven through Jesus paying the penalty of my sin and substituting Himself for me!

I laid on my bed that night thinking nothing had happened when, in fact, everything happened. As I called to Him, He acted, I was forgiven, saved from hell, given a completely new life and assured of a place in heaven. Now, more than 40 years on, I marvel at how God has lead me through a 39-year career in the Royal Air Force, from young apprentice through the Non-commissioned ranks and through Commissioned service. Looking back, I see clearly that the Lord has ordered my steps. He has taken me to places I would have avoided, yet blessed me in every one. He has prevented me from going to places I would have chosen, yet never let me be disappointed. I have failed Him aplenty yet He has never failed me once.

Until that day in RAF Ballykelly, I had been half-right. I was on my way to hell because I deserved to be there. Now I know the whole truth. I still do not deserve to go to heaven but God, in His love and Mercy, has reserved me a place through the sacrifice of His Son. "For God so loved the world, that He gave His only begotten Son, that whosoever believeth in Him should not perish, but have everlasting life" (John 3:16). What is more, He has promised one day to take me there. "In my Father's house are many mansions: if it were not so, I would have told you. I go to prepare a place for you. And if I go and prepare a place for you, I will come again, and receive you unto myself; that where I am, there ye may be also" (John 14:6).

Now, as General Secretary of SASRA, I seek to lead a dedicated team of evangelists and support workers to make known the good news of salvation to men and women in the Army and the Royal Air Force. There are many, like I used to be – searching for fulfillment and meaning in life. My desire is that they will discover Jesus as their best friend and saviour. If only they knew God and His Son Jesus all of life and whatever the future holds would become different.

The Bible reminds us in the book of *Hebrews 2:3*:

"how shall we escape if we ignore such a great salvation?

This salvation, which was first announced by the Lord, was confirmed to us by those who heard Him."

Sqn Ldr Woodland trained as an Aircraft Instrument Fitter. He served in Northern Ireland, Singapore and many units in the UK. He became General Secretary of SASRA in September, 2003 and lives with his wife Sharon, in Aldershot.

44

ASR Bill Woolfall MBE

At eleven years of age, I was asked by a girl friend to go with her on a church trip to hear Billy Graham in Manchester. At the close of the meeting, I responded to the invitation to go to the front. Within a few weeks however, I went back to my previous ways. I still believed in God but I was not living the Christian life.

In 1965 I left Liverpool and joined the ACC (Army Catering Corps). Within a year I married Pat and we had our first child Zena, some two years later. It was then that I decided that because I now had a family, I had better start doing 'Godly' things just in case God punished me or my family. I resolved to start reading one chapter of the Bible every day without fail, say my prayers and go to church. Then we had another child, Lisa, so still fearing I might not be doing enough for God, who might still punish me, I decided to read two chapters every day. The next child, Tara, upped it to three chapters, then David was four chapters every day, not missing one day in case something awful might happen. Although I read these chapters faithfully every day, I did not study the Bible and my daily prayers were mechanical; thank you for this or that and please help me pass this or that course; help me pass my exams and get my promotion to Warrant Officer. My focus was on God the Father and I knew little of the Lord Jesus Christ.

All this time we went as a family to church, even helping in Sunday School, yet I do not remember any preaching on repentance, forgiveness or commitment to Christ. If it was preached, I did not hear it and it did not touch my heart.

On my last of many unaccompanied tours to Northern Ireland, I was reading Corrie Ten Boom's book 'The Hiding Place' and I could not work out or understand if I was a Christian, and she undoubtedly was, why there was such a big difference in myself and her. It was not until Pat, who by this time had become a committed Christian, sent me the tract 'Journey into Life' that it all started to fall into place. I read the first page and realised that I was not a committed Christian

Pat had also asked our Chaplain, Graham Hadfield, to come and see me when he came on a visit to Northern Ireland. This he did and was able to answer my questions by taking me through the tract. As a result, I committed my life to Christ in November, 1984. Then I really felt the presence of Jesus, He was there at my right hand, I felt I could reach out and touch Him.

Then there was the growing and the learning and like all relationships with those you love, I wanted (and still do) to know more and more about Jesus.

After reading the Bible for all those years it had now become alive, it made sense, I really wanted to read, to talk to Jesus and to worship in church.

Some two years later from different sources I really believed that God was calling us into full time service, but I did not know what. I had lots of suggestions and after much prayer I eventually had two interviews. One with the Church Army and the other with SASRA. Neither Pat nor I wanted it to be with SASRA. I travelled overnight from Germany by car to attend the interviews but through a series of events I did not make the Church Army interview. Col Sear of SASRA interviewed me and although he thought that I had the gift of personal evangelism, he advised me that once I came out of the army I should get settled into a civilian church and come back in about five years time. I thought what he meant was 'Do not call us, we will call you!' I assumed that maybe I had it wrong. Perhaps full time service meant evangelising in the work place.

I came out of the Army in 1987 as a WO2 Master Chef. The growing process was continuing as God enabled me to submit to His will. Through all this we still had the sense that there was more. I just wanted to do what God wanted me to do and to be obedient to His command.

We bought our house in Tewkesbury, where I had a job with Cheltenham Borough Council as their Catering Manager. During this time because of what I felt, I became a Local Representative for SASRA. When we bought our house the mortgage rate was low and we worked out that my pension would cover that. However, the rates began to rise and rise, the payments far outweighed my pension and it came to a point where I really needed a better paid job. Out of the blue the Chief Catering Officer for Cheltenham left and I was asked to apply for the post to which I was appointed with a pay rise adequate to cover our mortgage. In this new post I quickly had to learn the tasks which the Army had not taught, like weekly and monthly accounts, wages, profit and loss, etc. Even with this new high powered job, I still did not feel I was in the right place.

At this time the Government's new policy of competitive tendering came in and our director was afraid that if we did put in a bid we might lose and in no time he would lose his staff. He put in a private bid with a contact insisting that present staff should be kept. All this happened and I was made General Area Manager of the South West. A grand sounding name but doing the same job.

On the face of it, everything was fine but I still felt that God wanted me to do more and in addition, things were happening that I felt were unethical.

The Saturday evening before Remembrance Day, the Managing Director telephoned and asked me to meet him for a breakfast on Sunday. I explained that due to the circumstances of the day, I would not be able to meet. He seemed quite satisfied with that. When I arrived at work on Monday, I was told that due to my lack of commitment to him and my commitment to God we should part company. I was devastated and had to clear my desk straight away. I was told to keep the car for a month and had a month's salary in lieu.

I arrived home mid-morning to find a letter

from Col Sear saying that, if I believed that God was still calling us into full time service, there was a post available at the 'Jackson Club,' Miss Daniell's Soldier's Home and also as a part time Scripture Reader. You can imagine how we felt. What an amazing God! We still had the car to come down and look over the place. Another amazing thing was that all the new skills I had learned in Cheltenham were needed in order to run the club, where our main aim is to serve. We have sensed the Lord's hand upon our lives. God has confirmed that we are in the right place, where He wants us to be.

Bill Woolfall joined the Army Catering Corps in 1965 and served in the regular Army until March, 1987. His ministry, along with that of Pat, his wife, began at the Jackson Club in January, 1991. He was awarded an MBE in the New Year's Honours list, 2004. Bill and Pat plan to retire from the Jackson Club during 2006.

45

ASR Derek Yarwood

When I joined the Army in 1957, I began to attend the Garrison Church in Canterbury. From this I moved to one of the well known denominations in Canterbury and for five years, wherever I was posted, I would attend this particular group.

Returning from leave in Northern Ireland to Shorncliffe, I found no one else in the Band Block. Whilst wondering what I should do, in walked ASR Harry Stickings, a person in the past I would have ignored. He walked straight up to me and invited me to a Billy Graham film to be shown at Victoria Hall, Hythe. Having nothing else to do I simply said, 'yes' and he arranged to meet me later on.

When we arrived at the Hall, it was packed so we had to sit at the back on a bench. The film was 'The Shadow of the Boomerang' and when it had finished a man got up at the front and asked that if anyone wanted to accept Christ as their Saviour, they should come forward. Being religious, I always thought I was a Christian. As I sat on the bench with a chair that had three vertical bars in front of me, God reminded me of the time when I had served a number of days in detention and on my cell door was a small square window with three vertical bars. I had paid the price for what I had done wrong and my slate was clean. Then God reminded me that Christ had died for me and paid the price for my sins. It was then that I realised that I needed Christ as my Saviour. There and then, I asked Christ to forgive me all my sins and to become my Saviour. I stood up and walked forward to the front. Standing there with me was an old soldier who had been a prisoner of war with the Japanese and he had just given his life to Jesus.

The Scripture Reader prayed with me and after the meeting was over he said, 'I want to give you a verse of Scripture' and he began to quote *2 Corinthians 5:17. 'Therefore if any man is in Christ, he is a new creature, the old things are passed away, behold, all things are become new'*. As soon as he had quoted this verse, the Holy Spirit revealed to me what I had really done. It was as if a light had been lit in my life. I knew Jesus as my Saviour for the first time in my life at the age of 21. I had been in bondage to religion for the past five years and now I was free from the penalty of sin. **PRAISE THE LORD!**

At this meeting was Barbara who had become a Christian in 1957 at a Billy Graham Crusade in London and within two years she was to become my wife.

I completed 23 years in the Army and the Lord called us both to serve Him with the Mission to Military Garrisons (MMG) in Benbecula. After completing a one year course at Glasgow Bible Training Institute, I joined Barbara who had been holding the fort whilst I was at college. I was then approached by Neil Innes, the Area Representative for Scotland, to become a part time Scripture Reader in Benbecula.

On completion of four years, the Mission sent us to Cyprus, where we stayed for seven years at Ayios Nikolaos as Superintendent and part time Scripture Reader. At the end of that time the Lord called Barbara and I to resign our position and return to the UK. Following this, I was called to spend a year at Moorlands Bible College and during which time I was part time Scripture Reader at Larkhill. Later we were called to full time ministry with SASRA.

Derek Yarwood served in the Regular Army from October, 1957 to December, 1980, firstly in the Royal Sussex Regiment and then in the Royal Army Ordinance Corps. His work as a part time Scripture Reader with SASRA began in December, 1981. He became a full time Reader in 1992.

46

Steps To Peace With God
By Billy Graham

Step 1 – God's Purpose: Peace and Life

God loves you and wants you to experience peace and life – abundant and eternal.

The Bible Says. . .

We have peace with God through our Lord Jesus Christ (Rom. 5:1).

For God so loved the world that He gave His only begotten Son, that whoever believes in Him should not perish but have everlasting life (John 3:16).

I have come that they may have life, and that they may have it more abundantly (John 10:10b).

Step 2 – Our Problem: Separation

God created us in His own image to have an abundant life. He did not make us as robots to automatically love and obey Him, but gave us a will and a freedom of choice.

We chose to disobey God and go our own wilful way. We still make this choice today. This results in separation from God.

The Bible Says. . .

For all have sinned and fall short of the glory of God (Rom. 3:23).

For the wages of sin is death, but the gift of God is eternal life in Christ Jesus our Lord (Rom. 6:23).

Our choice results in seperation from God.

People (Sinful)

God (Holy)

Our Attempts

Through the ages, individuals have tried in many ways to bridge this gap. . . without success. . .

The Bible Says. . .

There is a way that seems right to man, but in the end it leads to death (Prov. 14:12).

But your iniquities have separated you from God; and your sins have hidden His face from you, so that He will not hear (Is. 59:2).

There is only one remedy for
this problem of seperation.

Step 3 – God's Remedy: The Cross

Jesus Christ is the only answer to this problem. He died on the Cross and rose from the grave, paying the penalty for our sin and bridging the gap between God and people.

The Bible Says. . .

God is on one side and all the people on the other side, and Christ Jesus, Himself man, is between them to bring them together (1 Tim. 2:5)

For Christ also has suffered once for sins, the just for the unjust, that He might bring us to God (1 Pet. 3:18a).

But God demonstrates His own love for us in this: While we were still sinners, Christ died for us (Rom. 5:8).

God has provided the only way ...
we must make the choice ...

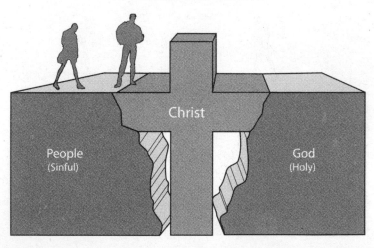

Step 4 – Our Response: Receive Christ

We must trust Jesus Christ and receive Him by personal invitation.

The Bible Says. . .

Behold, I stand at the door and knock. If anyone hears My voice and opens the door, I will come in to him and dine with him, and he with Me (Rev. 3:20).

But as many as received Him, to them He gave the right to become children of God, even to those who believe in His name (John 1:12).

If you confess with your mouth the Lord Jesus and believe in your heart that God has raised Him from the dead, you will be saved (Rom. 10:9).

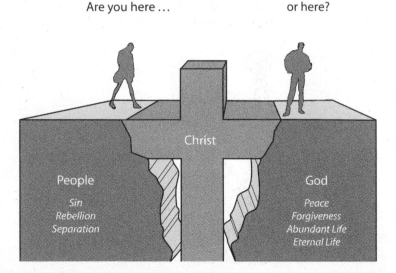

Is there any good reason why you
cannot receive Jesus Christ right now?

How to receive Christ:

1. *Admit your need (I am a sinner).*
2. *Be willing to turn from your sins (repent).*
3. *Believe that Jesus Christ died for you on the Cross
   and rose from the grave.*
4. *Through prayer, invite Jesus Christ to come in and
   control your life through the Holy Spirit. (Receive
   Him as Lord and Savior.)*

What to Pray:

Dear Lord Jesus,
*I know that I am a sinner and need Your forgiveness. I
believe that You died for my sins. I want to turn from
my sins. I now invite You to come into my heart and life.
I want to trust and follow You as Lord and Savior.
In Jesus' name. Amen.*

Date........................... Signature...

God's Assurance: His Word

If you prayed this prayer,

The Bible Says. . .

For 'whoever calls upon the name of the Lord will be saved' (Rom. 10:13).

Did you sincerely ask Jesus Christ to come into your life? Where is He right now? What has He given you?

For it is by grace you have been saved, through faith – and this is not from yourselves, it is the gift of God – not by works, so that no one can boast (Eph. 2:8, 9).

The Bible Says. . .

'He who has the Son has life; he who does not have the Son of God does not have life. These things I have written to you who believe in the name of the Son of God, that you may know that you have eternal life, and that you may continue to believe in the name of the Son of God' (1 John 5:12–13, NKJV).

Receiving Christ, we are born into God's family through the supernatural work of the Holy Spirit who indwells every believer. . . this is called regeneration or the 'new birth.'

This is just the beginning of a wonderful new life in Christ. To deepen this relationship you should:

1. *Read your Bible every day to know Christ better.*
2. *Talk to God in prayer every day.*
3. *Tell others about Christ.*
4. *Worship, fellowship, and serve with other Christians in a church where Christ is preached.*
5. *As Christ's representative in a needy world, demonstrate your new life by your love and concern for others.*

God bless you as you do.

Billy Graham

If you want further help in the decision you have made, write to:

S.A.S.R.A.
Havelock House, Barrack Road,
Aldershot, Hants. GU11 3NP

www.sasra.org.uk

e-mail: info@sasra.org.uk

Glossary

ACC	Army Catering Corps
ARCM	Associate of the Royal College of Music
ARRC	Associate of Royal Red Cross
ASR	Army Scripture Reader
Brig	Brigadier
CAMus	Corps of Army Music
Capt	Captain
CB	Companion of the Order of the Bath
CBE	Commander of the Order of the British Empire
CCF	College Cadet Force
Gen	General
LRAM	Licentiate of the Royal Academy of Music
Lt Col	Lieutenant Colonel
LDOS	Lord's Day Observance Society
Maj Gen	Major General

MBE	Member of the Order of the British Empire
MC	Military Cross
MMG	Mission To Military Garrisons
NAAFI	Naval Army and Air Force Institutes
OCU	Officers' Christian Union
Our Day	SASRA Annual Meetings
POW	Prisoner of War
QARANC	Queen Alexandra's Royal Army Nursing Corps
RAMC	Royal Army Medical Corps
RMA	Royal Military Academy
RSM	Regimental Sergeant Major
RSME	Royal School of Military Engineering
RUC	Royal Ulster Constabulary
SACA	Soldiers' and Airmen's Christian Association
SASRA	The Soldiers' and Airmen's Scripture Readers Association
Sgt	Sergeant
S/Sgt	Staff Sergeant
Sqn Ldr	Squadron Leader
TA	Territorial Army
TSR	Travelling Scripture Reader
UDR	Ulster Defence Regiment

VE Day	Victory in Europe
WRAF	Women's Royal Air Force
YMCA	Young Men's Christian Association